Getting Your Foot in the Door

When You Don't Have a Leg to Stand On

Rob Sullivan

Contemporary Books

Chicago   New York   San Francisco   Lisbon   London   Madrid   Mexico City
Milan   New Delhi   San Juan   Seoul   Singapore   Sydney   Toronto

Library of Congress Cataloging-in-Publication Data

Sullivan, Rob (Robert Ryan), 1967–
    Getting your foot in the door when you don't have a leg to stand on / Rob Sullivan.
       p.   cm.
    Includes bibliographical references.
    ISBN 0-8092-2340-6
    1. Job hunting.   2. Vocational guidance.   I. Title.

HF5382.7.S853   2001
650.14—dc21   2001037139

Contemporary Books 🖋

*A Division of The **McGraw·Hill** Companies*

1 2 3 4 5 6 7 8 9 0   AGM/AGM   0 9 8 7 6 5 4 3 2 1

ISBN 0-8092-2340-6

This book was set in Rotis Serif
Printed and bound by Quebecor Martinsburg

Cover and interior design by Amy Yu Ng
Cover illustrations copyright © Geoff Smith/Images.com, Inc.

McGraw-Hill books are available at special quantity discounts to use as premiums and sales promotions, or for use in corporate training programs. For more information, please write to the Director of Special Sales, Professional Publishing, McGraw-Hill, Two Penn Plaza, New York, NY 10121-2298. Or contact your local bookstore.

This book is printed on acid-free paper.

This book is dedicated to the undiscovered and underappreciated artists and musicians of the world. This long list includes, but is not limited to:

Chuck Brodsky ■ Ralph Covert & The Bad Examples ■ Dave Crossland ■ Kat Eggleston ■ eddie from ohio ■ Brother Mark Elder ■ Gertrude ■ Stewart Harris ■ Michael Lille ■ The Mary Janes ■ Matthew Moon ■ The Nadas ■ The Otters ■ Tracy Lynn Pristas ■ Ryan Tracy Band ■ Sons of the Never Wrong ■ Speidel, Goodrich, Goggin & Lille ■ The Vulgar Boatmen ■ Harry Wilson

Contents

Acknowledgments vii

From the Author ix

Introduction xi

1   The Job Search Process 1

2   Finding the Jobs 10

3   The Self-Assessment 30

4   Redefining the Résumé 57

5   Cover Letters 97

6   Interviews 116

7   Analyzing an Interviewer's Questions 142

8   Following Up and Closing the Deal 163

9   Improving Your Technique and Yourself 174

Recommended Reading 184

Acknowledgments

Only within the last few years have I seen my "fiercely independent" nature as a weakness rather than a strength. As a result, I have only begun to recognize, accept, and acknowledge the contributions others make to my life. You (the readers of this book) and I will never fully appreciate the extent to which professionals, friends, and family added insight to this project. But I assure you, we are both better for it. Although space constraints prohibit me from mentioning everyone who challenged me, coached me, inspired me, encouraged me, made me smile, or surprised me along the way, I remain eternally grateful to every one of them.

In the interest of brevity, I limit my specific achknowledgments to the people who worked on this project on a day-to-day basis. First and foremost, I'd like to thank my editor, Denise Betts, who came up with some absolutely fabulous suggestions to transform this book into what it is today. Even more amazing, Denise made the process fun. I actually looked forward to her comments and our conversations because of the way she constantly inspired me. I also owe a tremendous debt of gratitude to Jane Jordan Browne, Scott Mendel, and everyone at Multimedia Product Development, Inc., the most supportive and enthusiastic agents ever. It's truly an honor to be represented by their team. Without the encouragement and support of these fine people, this book would not be in your hands right now.

I also extend my sincere appreciation to the McGraw-Hill editorial and sales team who came up with the title.

And, of course, special thanks to my mom, dad, sisters (ML and Clare), and brothers (Bill, John, and Matt)—the best family anyone could have. Without their encouragement, generosity, and patience, this book would not exist.

From the Author

In my life, I have learned that at precisely those times when life seems to get worse that you may actually be getting ready to make a leap. When you feel like you're getting nowhere—stagnating, even slipping backward—what you're actually doing is backing up to get a running start   —*Dan Millman,* **Sacred Journey of the Peaceful Warrior**

Dear Future Executive:

My reasons for writing this book are both personal and professional. Although I have always enjoyed writing, I limited myself to an occasional song, poem, or letter. I never thought about writing a book. Like many of life's great opportunities, this book had more to do with timing than planning.

Over the past few years, I have received a steady stream of calls from people who needed help job hunting. For the most part, they had what it takes to succeed. They just didn't realize it. After spending countless hours working one-on-one with these people, the need for this book became clear. It is my effort to share with the professionals of tomorrow what I have learned from the executives of today. This is the book that would have made my own job search easier.

If you look at job hunting as a numbers game, the odds weigh heavily against you. Companies receive thousands of unsolicited résumés every year. Many also recruit at top colleges, universities, and business schools. This competition can be fierce, but it isn't always well-prepared. With a focused, strategic effort, a B.A. who demonstrates potential can compete successfully—even against people with advanced degrees and work experience. Simply put, the ability to market yourself effectively can be far more valuable than an advanced degree.

It would be a mistake to view this book as a one-size-fits-most, fill-in-the-blanks career guide. You won't find shortcuts or easy answers. Instead, you will discover strategies to market yourself effectively. You don't have to love marketing. And you don't have to make a career of it. But you do have to be good at it. Otherwise, your dream job will be just that—a dream.

Job hunting does not have to be difficult. You don't have to pretend to be someone you're not. You might think you need full-time experience, an internship at a Fortune 500 company, or a network of executive contacts, but you don't. Those fall strictly in the "nice-to-have" category. You already have the only asset you need—potential.

Best of luck in landing the job of your dreams!

Rob

Introduction

> The basis of optimism is sheer terror.
> —*Oscar Wilde*
>
> There's never time to do it right. But there's always time to do it over.
> —*Unknown*

With legions of college students entering the work force every year, competition for entry level jobs is intense. A college degree simultaneously qualifies its holder for everything and nothing. In this sense, the degree is invaluable and worthless. As my grandmother puts it, "Your diploma and a bus token will get you downtown."

When it comes to job hunting, college and graduate students probably need the most help. They are also least likely to receive it. Unfortunately, society does more to help nonprofessionals than it does to help the educated. Vocational high schools, secretarial schools, and truck driving schools are but a few of the limitless options available to the American working class. These schools, which often have close relationships with potential employers, provide helpful job placement services as well as education. The same is not always true for students and job hunters who pursue corporate or professional careers.

> Worldly wisdom teaches that it is better for the reputation to fail conventionally than to succeed unconventionally.
>
> —*John Maynard Keynes*

What we lack is an effective way to help educated people pursue executive positions. The message is silent but clear: "You're smart enough to be where you are, figure it out yourself."

In the absence of effective training, aspiring professionals must rely on natural ability, luck, and resourcefulness. As a result, a disproportionate number of graduates accept jobs that are not the best match for their interests and abilities. Fortunately, there's hope. By recognizing and demonstrating your potential, you can learn to market yourself effectively.

This book is based on the theory that your relationship with a potential employer is almost exactly the same as the relationships that exist between products and consumers. There is only one key difference: in the job search, you are both product and salesperson. Playing both roles may seem difficult at times, but with a clear, strategic focus and an unwavering belief in yourself, you will find the process can be quite rewarding.

The job seekers most likely to benefit from this book have already focused on a particular career—whatever that may be. If this describes you, congratulations. You are taking the right steps. The fact that you are reading this suggests that you are eager to learn and willing to challenge yourself. These are valuable qualities to any employer when you know how to present them.

If you read this book passively, if you merely nod your head occasionally and then put it away, you will have wasted your time. Treat it as a textbook. Give yourself homework assignments. Scribble notes in the margin. You are both teacher and student. Although this book requires effort and self-discipline, I have included questions and examples to help you prepare.

What If I Have No Idea What I Want to Do?

If you find yourself in this category, there are a few issues to address before you begin. Start by asking friends and family what they could see you doing for a career. You may be surprised to discover that your talents are more apparent to loved ones than they are to you. Although it might seem strange, it is perfectly normal. For years, these people have probably been encouraging you to develop your talents. And if you are anything like me, you've been ignoring them.

All my life, teachers, friends, and family have encouraged me to write. Anytime anyone suggested that I write a book, I disregarded the suggestion with my usual comment, "If I had anything worth saying, I would." Of course, I not so secretly believed I didn't have anything worth saying. Like so many people, I had a tendency to devalue myself.

Fortunately, there is another soul-searching exercise that can uncover your hidden talents. Just ask yourself what it is that people need when they seek your assistance or advice. If you aren't sure, start paying attention. Over the next few weeks or months keep a journal and make a note anytime someone asks for your assistance. You may be surprised with what you discover.

In my case, it was my perseverance in the job search process that caught the attention of people who knew me. Upon hearing how many rejections I encountered while pursuing my ideal field, in which I had no practical experience, more than a few people told me they would have given up long before. Without my realizing or intending it, my perseverance and eventual success inspired people. Nevertheless, it still took me over five years to accept the fact that I had developed a base of knowledge worth sharing. Until that point, the only people who benefited were those who actively sought my assistance.

Whatever you do, don't automatically jump to any conclusions about whether you can make money pursuing a particular career. There are countless people who make a living doing what they love. If you're looking for inspiration along these lines, there are two books you should read. The first, *Do What You Love and the Money Will Follow*, by Marsha Sinetar, is a wonderful book that examines, in depth, the obstacles and opportunities that arise when people pursue careers that are in sync with their values and interests. The second, *Entrepreneurs Are Made, Not Born*, by Lloyd Shefsky, contains over two hundred case histories of successful entrepreneurs. Both of these books are incredibly inspiring and thought provoking.

Case Studies

Throughout the book, you will find case studies from a variety of different industries. While the needs of each employer will differ, the basic principles of marketing still apply when it comes to selling yourself as a product. There is simply no substitute for knowing how to position yourself relative to your competition. By understanding and using the principles outlined in the following chapters, you will be better able to compete for the most sought after jobs in the world, in a competitive marketplace, and against others who may have more practical experience.

We will also explore how you can reposition yourself to appeal to companies with completely different needs. In other words, you will learn how to modify the approach to match your talents to your area of interest. With a few weeks of focused preparation, you can sell yourself into almost any job. Why? Because that is a few weeks longer than the competition usually spends.

Traps to Avoid

When the economy is good, the tendency for many is to take shortcuts in the job search process. For example, people who otherwise would spend time researching a company will instead throw together a generic cover letter and hope for the best. When there are more jobs than good people to fill them, you might land a few interviews this way. However, I would strongly encourage you not to do this. No matter how great or poor the economy is, you have to take responsibility for your long-term happiness by thoroughly researching each potential employer. Don't let laziness play a role. Instead, when you're faced with a wide range of options, use the strategies in this book and take the time to make an informed decision. The more time you spend doing this, the less likely it is that you'll find yourself facing unpleasant surprises on the job.

Marketing Yourself and Developing a Personal Marketing Plan

Despite what you might think, your ability to get a job has little to do with experience or intelligence. You don't need a résumé overflowing with internships and degrees. And it isn't necessarily about being in the right place at the right time—although that never hurts. Instead, getting the job you want is about taking the time to learn to market yourself. This is a lifelong process with serious short- and long-term implications. After all, your experience with each job and each passing year is cumulative. Even if you change careers, you will still have accumulated skills and knowledge that enhance your value, though it might not directly relate to your current or desired position.

To market yourself effectively, you must match your skills with the needs of a potential employer. This way, the job search can be quick and relatively painless. On the other hand, if you don't know what the company needs, you probably don't know what you have to offer. In this case, you will be relying on luck to guide your personal and professional satisfaction. This is a simple recipe for disappointment. Worse, your job search will drag on indefinitely until you give up and accept a position for which you are overqualified.

A marketing plan—whether it's for a person, product, or service—must include a thorough analysis of the product, the consumer or target audience, the industry or category, and the competition. In the job search, you are the product; the potential employer is the consumer; your cover letter and résumé are interest-generating print ads; and your interview is the sales call in which both parties assess whether the product (you) fits the consumer's needs (the available position).

In some cases there are significant differences between companies with respect to the qualities they seek. Take time to identify these differences because your value will be measured by your ability to meet the needs of the employer.

Without a personal marketing plan, most candidates make the hiring decision an easy one. They have no idea what the company needs or what they, as candidates, have to offer. Some don't even know why they want to work in a given field. With so many other people competing for the same position, no interviewer has time to search for a spark of potential. It must be immediately apparent. Of those who don't succeed, few ever find out why. Most people don't even think to ask.

Ongoing Efforts

Just as the marketing effort does not end when a customer makes a purchase decision, your marketing effort should not end when you get an offer or rejection. The challenge has just begun.

The first and most important challenges you will face on the job involve both personal and professional development and customer satisfaction. The customers, in this case, are your employer and your clients or corporate customers who count on you to perform whatever job they hired you to do.

While you may be fortunate to participate in a formal training program, it doesn't change the fact that your professional development is ultimately up to you. For this reason, one of your most important challenges is to identify at least one mentor who can help guide your career.

From a practical standpoint, it may take time before you begin having a positive, measurable impact on your employer's business. But it also isn't unheard of for people to make valuable contributions starting on their first day. Whatever the case, start a work journal in which you keep a record of your ideas and contributions. For every project, ask yourself, "How is the outcome different (preferably better) because I was involved?" I like to think of this as the *It's a Wonderful Life* approach to marketing yourself on the job.

Beyond Rejection

Unfortunately, the best preparation may not spare you from disappointment. Should this happen, keep looking for opportunities to improve upon your presentation, whether that be your résumé, cover letter, or interviewing skills. Never stop believing in yourself. This is an active process. As a wise person once said: "Disappointment is when you only hope things get better."

Whatever you do, don't take rejection personally. Instead, treat it as the learning experience it is. Later on we'll look at specific strategies you can use to learn from rejection. In the meantime maintain a positive attitude and keep your eyes focused on your goal. Most important, keep your mind and heart open as we look into the past to better understand the person you are today and how that relates to the needs of potential employers.

The Job Search Process

It's never wise to leap a chasm in two bounds. —*Chinese Proverb*

Every moment spent planning saves two or three moments of execution.
—*Hyrum Smith (attributed)*

job. I found myself in the same position when I first graduated from college, and the mistakes I made were not unusual. With solid preparation, a willingness to learn from rejection, and the insight to know how to handle the competition, you can save yourself from much of the pain I experienced and compete successfully in the job market.

The primary purpose of this chapter is to provide an overview of the job search process, highlighting the steps people are most likely to miss. Every day, job hunters send résumés, embark on interviews, receive rejections, and wonder why they're having so much trouble landing a

The Paradox of Preparation

It's always amazed me that people will spend several hundred dollars and weeks of their lives taking SAT, LSAT, and GMAT preparation courses, but won't spend more than a weekend on cover letters, résumés, and interview preparation. The other tactical error that people make is to treat the job search as a black and white proposition—either they get the job or they don't. Sadly, this ignores the enormous distinction between just missing the cut and never coming close.

A rejection is not the job market's way of saying you aren't good enough. A rejection is nothing more than a warning that you aren't marketing yourself effectively. If you don't heed the warnings and uncover opportunities for improvement, you will repeat the same mistakes. Instead, you need to find out why you didn't get the job, and adjust your job search efforts accordingly.

The typical scenario

You interview. You wait. You think about calling. You wait a little longer. Finally, you call. The company has no news. A few weeks pass. At last a postcard arrives:

> *Thank you for expressing an interest in our company. Unfortunately, your background and abilities do not match our needs at this time. Best of luck in your job search.*

If you're a college student, a letter like this is usually good for a free beer at the campus pub. On the other hand, if you're in the middle of an extensive job search, this may be one more in an unbroken string of rejections. Either way, it says nothing more than, "You didn't get the job."

Although it would be nice if employers took the time to share constructive feedback with candidates who aren't hired, it almost never happens. Instead, unsuccessful applicants are left to examine their efforts themselves, in order to improve upon their presentation the next time around. There are several reasons for this lack of feedback. First, most applicants either don't think to ask or prefer the ostrich method of job hunting, where they keep their heads firmly in the sand, oblivious to the opinions of others. A second and equally important reason is a legal one.

In our litigious and vengeful society, there is a tendency to couch every phrase in the most nebulous and inoffensive terms. As a result, the most common explanation for rejections (i.e., "Your talents don't meet our needs") is meaningless.

Another approach

Given the intense competition in the job market, it's unrealistic to expect that you or anyone else can avoid rejection. I didn't, no one I know did, and you probably won't either. Instead, your probability for success is a function of your willingness to extract value from rejection and failure. Putting your ego on the line—particularly in front of a company that has already rejected you—probably seems like a stressful and time-consuming diversion. What makes this approach worthwhile is the impact it can have on your effectiveness.

From Here to Your Future

When the distance between your present situation and your goals is measured in time, the shortest distance is not always a straight line. A jagged route may be the shortest. Consider the following diagram:

A ——————— B ——————— C ——————— D
(unemployment)   (sending résumés   (interviewing)   (ideal job)
                 & cover letters)

If point A is unemployment and point D is your dream job, the straight line between A and D, with the requisite stops for cover letters, résumés, and interviewing, would seem to be the shortest path. If you are already proficient at marketing yourself, perhaps it is. Otherwise, it most definitely is not.

Without preparation and practice, a straight line between A and D cannot exist. A more accurate visual representation looks like this:

A   C ——————— D ——————— E
(unemployment)   (sending résumés   (interviewing)   (ideal job)
                 & cover letters)

B
(preparation: self-analysis &
marketing plan)

Your journey from unemployment to your ideal position, must include a thorough self-analysis and a personal marketing plan. If there was a way to avoid these steps, someone would have found it by now. Instead, people think they know what they want to do in their career, but when questioned, they have difficulty articulating why they want to do it. Fewer still are able to construct a convincing argument for why they would be good at whatever career they have chosen. Job hunters of all ages and experience levels fall into this trap.

No matter where you are in your career, your challenge as a job hunter is to convince an employer that you have the potential to succeed in a given position. To do so, you must know how the employer assesses potential. This is where your *personal marketing plan* comes into play.

The personal marketing plan expands your self-analysis to include an analysis of the company and the competition you will face as a job hunter. With this foundation, you will be better able to construct an intelligent selling message that can convince the company of your potential.

In this case, the shortest distance between point A and point F is:

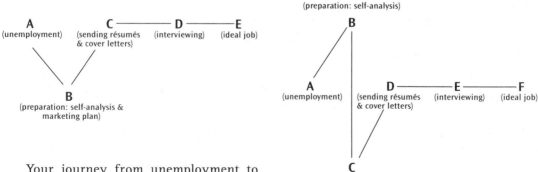

(preparation: self-analysis)
B

A   D ——————— E ——————— F
(unemployment)   (sending résumés   (interviewing)   (ideal job)
                 & cover letters)

C
(personal marketing plan)

When distance is measured in time, or as a function of the probability for success, the following is true:

$$AB + BC + CD + DE + EF < AF$$

Fortunately, this is almost all the math you need to know. So, if you're an English or social science major, have no fear!

If this concept is confusing, there's another way you can look at it. Jim Muccio, founder of Simulation Support, Inc., compared this to a physics principle known as "least time." Although least time relates to the way light moves through objects like glass or water, it's not difficult to grasp.

Imagine that you were standing on the edge of a river with no current, and you saw someone about 150 feet to your left and 100 feet from shore who was starting to drown. If you jumped in to save the person from where you were standing, you'd have to swim on a diagonal until you were out 100 feet from shore and about 150 feet to the left of where you started. That might be the shortest distance, but it certainly would not be the fastest route. Since most people can run faster than they can swim, it would take less time to run 150 feet down the riverbank and swim 100 feet straight out to the victim. Running the extra 150 feet adds distance, but it also shortens the actual time it takes to make the journey. The time invested in doing a thorough self-analysis and personal marketing plan has the same impact on the journey from unemployment to your ideal job. These two extra steps make the journey shorter and far more enjoyable.

An ounce of preparation . . .

I'm not going to deceive you into believing that there are effective shortcuts when it comes to the job search process. There aren't. But remember, this is the work that will set you apart from the people who want the same job you do. With very few exceptions, most of those who struggle in their job search do so because they haven't prepared. They don't really know who they are, what they want to do, why they'd be good at it, what a potential employer is looking for, or how they might add value to a particular organization. These aren't simple issues. However, they are accessible to everyone with a modicum of effort.

The commitment you must make to preparation may not excite you. You may envision many long, tedious hours of self-examination and assessments that would make a psychology student's head spin, but it's better than the alternative—settling for the wrong job.

Your Competition

To compete effectively in the job market, you must understand the relative strengths of the types of people pursuing the same job. You don't need to know the names, past employers, and alma maters of each candidate. What's important to know is the kind of people you'll be up against. Do they have advanced degrees? Have they worked in the industry? What do these people offer that you don't? What are your strengths relative

> If you compare yourself with others, you may become vain or bitter, for always there will be greater and lesser persons than yourself.
>
> —*Desiderata*

to the competition? This information is essential if you hope to position yourself effectively.

Recent college graduates

Some companies prefer to hire candidates with bachelor's degrees because they have lower starting salaries than candidates with advanced degrees. Depending on the candidate, some recent grads are also more energetic and eager to learn. Without full-time corporate experience, these candidates are seen as blank slates that can be shaped, molded, and trained to the company's specifications.

On the down side, there are more and more young people, with and without advanced degrees, who approach potential employers with what can only be described as a bizarre sense of entitlement. It is as if these candidates expect to bypass the entry level and proceed directly to middle management. This is neither realistic nor appropriate. There are no shortcuts to proving yourself. For these reasons, it's perfectly appropriate for entry-level candidates to highlight their willingness to work hard to succeed.

To people with a good, old-fashioned work ethic, it seems almost incomprehensible that there would be a need to point out a willingness to work hard, but it's become an important selling point because so many people lack this trait. As an interviewer, it's also refreshing to hear, so don't be afraid to mention it. Among employers and recruiters all over the country, there is also serious concern about the work ethic of the younger members of the work force. Fewer people are willing to put in the time and effort people once willingly sacrificed to get ahead.

I have mixed feelings about this. On the one hand, our country has long had a reputation for working people too hard with too little time for vacation. Some entry-level employees are fortunate to get any vacation at all. Those who do get vacation rarely start with more than two weeks. Meanwhile, our friends overseas routinely get a month or more. While that strikes me as a lot healthier, I don't have any delusions that European ideals will be adopted here anytime soon.

Positioning yourself against the competition

At some point, you may encounter an interviewer who challenges your level of education relative to other candidates. Should this happen, focus on what you have to offer. Avoid direct comparisons between your level of education and another. If you're asked specifically for a comparison, highlight the positive. Whatever you do, don't answer the question, "Why shouldn't we hire them?" Instead, answer the question, "Why should we hire you?" Companies hire "them" all the time.

Being clear on the relative merits of your education is particularly important if you have an advanced degree. If the company will be paying you a premium salary, know why you are worth it, and go in prepared to explain it in detail.

Rapid promotion pitfalls

For the past few years, the economy has been such that qualified applicants are harder to find than open positions. Think of it as a big game of musical chairs. If the music stopped and everyone found his or her perfect job, there would still be plenty of empty chairs. In a hopeless effort to fill open positions, many companies have been forced to promote people well before they are truly ready. Unfortunately, this is a Band-Aid solution that isn't in the long-term best interest of anyone.

From an individual perspective, rapid promotion is definitely something to be conscious of because it isn't reasonable to expect that the advancement brought about by the strong job market will continue for your entire career. At the same time, it's only natural to believe you're capable of more than you've been trained to do simply because you've been promoted or given a particular title.

A candidate I recently encountered faced exactly this dilemma. With a strong personal presentation and a stellar educational background, Jeff sold himself into a variety of different positions. Having spent no more than two years at any one place, he never had an opportunity to develop as a manager. Nevertheless, Jeff used his considerable charm and poise to convince a company to hire him at a very senior level. Unfortunately for everyone involved, it was a disaster. Within months, the people who reported to Jeff got together and approached the president with an ultimatum: "Fire Jeff or we quit!" That's about as straightforward as it gets.

Even though the company managed to counsel Jeff out of the job, he never stopped believing that he was at the appropriate level. This denial, no doubt, was also a function of his overall business immaturity. Nothing could convince him to take a step back, focus on developing as a manager, and advance without limit. Instead, he spent the next year unemployed and searching for a senior management position.

Unfortunately, Jeff is not the only casualty of premature promotion and inflated personal expectations. The lesson to be learned from his experience is to find a mentor who can help you understand what it truly takes to succeed in any given field. It's the best way I know to avoid the pitfalls that await unsuspecting, naive professionals.

From a job hunting perspective, it's important to have a thorough understanding of the job specifications and responsibilities before you apply. Considering that candidates rarely meet all the requirements for any given position, companies prioritize and decide on a case by case basis where and how they can be flexible. If you meet most but not all of the important requirements, don't sell yourself short by not applying. Instead, be upfront about whatever requirements you're missing, and do your best to balance them with valuable qualities the prospective employer might not have mentioned.

> Only passions, great passions, can elevate the soul to great things.
> —*Denis Diderot*
>
> We may become the makers of our fate when we have ceased to pose as its prophets. —*Karl Popper*

What you don't want to do is pretend you've done something you haven't. For example, let's imagine a company is looking to hire someone who has at least ten years of management experience supervising twenty to forty people. If the job seems perfect in all respects except that you've been in management less than five years and supervised no more than three people, there may be an alternative. In the interest of letting executives handpick their teams, companies often hire from the top down. In this case, the company may be recruiting for the highest position within the department, knowing that other positions also need to be filled. For this reason, it would make sense to put together a cover letter explaining your interest in the company

and being forthright about your level of experience.

By acknowledging the company's need for someone with more experience, you basically give management the option to consider you for a less senior position. If the hiring manager likes your background enough, he or she may decide to rethink the original requirements. Either way, you win. And if it doesn't work out, you haven't lost anything either.

Creating Awareness

When launching a new product or service, companies often rely on the power of advertising. Whether they use a print ad, commercial, sales brochure, or billboard, the goal is the same—to generate interest. Your résumé and cover letter are no different. You are the product, and the prospective employer is the consumer. Your goal is to generate interviews and job offers.

Let's start with cover letters, résumés, and interviews. As we move ahead and explore these in detail, you may discover, as many people have, that some of your difficulty in the job search process has been the result of an incorrect or incomplete understanding of these terms. Before we discuss them, it might be helpful to explore the feelings you associate with these terms. This might sound strange, but if you don't take the time to confront fear, apprehension, or similarly unhelpful states-of-mind, they will continue to hinder your progress. By taking the time to understand and deal with your emotions, your job search won't be a humbling, ego-battering experience.

Unprovoked Feelings

How do you feel when you hear someone mention cover letters, résumés, and interviews? Does the mere thought of putting together a cover letter or résumé send you into immediate writer's block? Does the prospect of looking for a job seem more like begging?

The feelings of inadequacy you may experience when it comes to presenting yourself are perfectly normal. Some people may hide it better than others, but almost everyone experiences it to some degree. The reason is simple: from a very early age, most of us are taught not to talk about ourselves.

If you spend time with young children, you will hear them talk unselfconsciously about how great they are in art, math, spelling, and any other subject they enjoy. What's more, kids are naturally great at self-promotion. They will say things like "Well, I'm great in math, I don't like history much, I'm okay in spelling, I love recess, and sometimes I talk to my neighbors too much." They are honest and open about their skills and achievements. And many of these same children will also tell anyone willing to listen where they need extra help.

Unfortunately, this inclination of children to express themselves is often suppressed by parents, teachers, and other adults, who discourage them. This is unfortunate because society's effort to keep children humble causes us to miss a wonderful opportunity to build self-esteem.

We often go from elementary through high school with our parents and teachers speaking for us. Not until our first job cover letter, résumé, or interview do we have to talk about our interests, abilities, strengths, or weaknesses. Little wonder it becomes such an issue. Without practice, almost everything feels unnatural. If this scenario is the origin of whatever insecurity you have about presenting yourself, take time to examine it before you forge ahead with your job search.

How do you see yourself?

Often, people who have issues with insecurity see themselves as inept, inadequate, unqualified, unreliable, or unfocused. Conversely, people with high self-esteem see themselves as smart, curious, resourceful, inventive, open, intuitive, optimistic, willing to learn, and coachable. Our thoughts about ourselves have an uncanny way of becoming self-fulfilling prophecies. As you think it, so shall it be.

If you have a tendency toward pessimism and negativity, I suggest you read *Learned Optimism*, by Martin Seligman. Much of the traditional research on success has focused on motivation and ability, but according to Seligman, a prominent psychologist, optimism may be an even more important factor in the success of any individual.

Seligman describes how optimism can be measured and used to predict success in the workplace. After more than twenty years of research, he has devised a survey to measure what he refers to as "explanatory style." This is the way an individual understands, interprets, and responds to a given event. According to this approach, an event is neither good nor bad, it just is. The positive or negative interpretation is a subjective, human element that has little or nothing to do with the event itself.

It's hardly surprising that Seligman found fundamental differences in the way optimists and pessimists explain unfavorable events. However, optimists and pessimists also differ significantly in the way they interpret favorable events.

> Whether you think you can or you think you can't, you're right.
>
> —*Unknown*
>
> When I look back on all these worries I remember the story of the old man who said on his deathbed that he had had a lot of trouble in his life, most of which had never happened.
>
> —*Sir Winston Churchill*

Explanatory Style

A person who thinks in absolute terms is said to have a pessimistic explanatory style. For example, everyone has heard people say, "Things never work out for me," or "I always make the same mistakes." In this way, the pessimist maintains a "this is the way it is" mentality about unfavorable circumstances. When good things happen to pessimists, they explain it away as luck. As a result, a pessimist expects life to quickly return to a more negative status quo.

In contrast, optimists are more likely to attribute success to hard work and natural ability. This optimistic attitude is valuable from a psychological standpoint—even when the facts don't justify such a positive self-assessment. In effect, this is a rare glimpse at the positive aspects of the self-fulfilling prophecy.

The good news about explanatory style in particular and optimism in general is that you can train yourself to think and behave differently. Many people paralyze themselves with pessimistic outlooks, but you don't necessarily have to be one of them.

Now that we've examined some of the common pitfalls that people encounter, it's time to identify the companies you want to target in your job search. In the next chapter, we'll examine a few strategies to identify and gather information about potential employers. The more you know, the easier it will be to sell yourself. Conversely, the less you know, the less likely it is that an employer will add you to the company team.

Finding the Jobs

> Not 16 percent of the human race is, or ever has been, engaged in any of the kinds of activity at which they excel.
>
> —*Mairet*

Comparing Companies

Knowing which career path you want to pursue does not lessen the effort required for analyzing the industry and learning everything you can about potential employers. At the same time, you need a solid grasp of the differences and similarities between companies to convince interviewers that you have done your homework. This is important because any company, in any industry, wants to hire people who have taken the time to learn about the company and the requirements of the position. The more educated you are about the position, the more attractive you will be to an employer. Conversely, the less you know about the company and the job requirements, the less attractive you will be.

As you compare and contrast companies, consider the following factors:

- What are the company's recruiting objectives?
- How large or small is the company?

- What is the company's reputation in its field?
- Who are the company's clients? What products or services does the company offer?

Recruiting objectives

Even within the same industry, different companies have different recruiting objectives. Although two companies may handle the same types of products or services, differences (e.g., clients) will always exist. This impacts the corporate culture and, ultimately, staffing requirements.

In preparing this book, I conducted an informal telephone survey of advertising recruiters. For the most part, these people didn't consider their objectives unusual. Nevertheless, the differences were extreme. The qualities sought by one agency might be meaningless—even detrimental—in the eyes of another.

In some cases, the differences can be attributed to the company's expectations about the future of the industry. One CEO described the perfect entry-level account person as creative and entrepreneurial. She based her preferences on the rapid changes already impacting her clients. In order to properly service these clients, she actively recruits risk-takers. In contrast, agencies with more conservative clients are often more risk-averse.

Note, however, that while it is possible to tailor your presentation to address companies with conflicting requirements, denying your preferences to gain employment is shortsighted and hazardous.

Clarify the company's objectives

The first and best place to find information on a particular company is usually the Internet. If the company has taken the time to think through exactly what it values in an employee, you'll probably find it on its website. However, if the website information is vague—and it often is—make phone calls rather than assumptions. First, call the human resources department and tell them you're interested in learning more about a position at their company. More specifically, you want to find out what qualities the company looks for in whatever position you seek. For example, if you are a recent college graduate, ask about specific entry-level positions. You might also ask the human resources contact if the company has a brochure that describes its recruiting objectives. Generally speaking, though, if human resources personnel have taken the time to put together a comprehensive brochure, they probably have the same information on their website, so check there first.

If the company doesn't have the information you're looking for, politely ask if there is there anyone—perhaps a first-year employee—who might be able to answer a few questions. Be sure to state upfront that you will only take a moment of the person's time.

Size of the company

Size is relative. To one person, a large but close-knit family atmosphere may seem small relative to a multibillion dollar global company. To another, it might seem enormous. For this reason, I will not attempt to establish artificial cutoff points between small, midsize, and large companies. Concerning size, the correct choice is the one that appeals to you.

If you are in the process of landing your first job, a large company can be a great opportunity for a number of reasons. First, you'll probably meet and interact with more people across more departments than in a small company. From a professional development standpoint, this is wonderful because it gives you the opportunity to learn how to work with a wider range of personalities in a relatively short period of time. The value of this experience should not be underestimated. From a purely social standpoint, the people you meet at a large company may ease your transition if you find yourself in a city where you don't know too many people.

If you've taken the time to follow the steps outlined in this book and you've landed what would seem to be the perfect job, the last thought in your mind will probably be your next career move. Nevertheless, the size and reputation of your first employer may be a major factor in your career path. People who have worked for large, well-known companies often have an advantage in the job market solely because of the reputation of the company. For example, if the company has a reputation

for hiring only the best, and you stay long enough to earn a promotion or two, it says a lot about who you are and what you can do. There is also a perception—not necessarily warranted—that large companies have good training programs. Therefore, other companies in the same industry will often actively recruit people who work at the larger companies.

In contrast, you might have an absolutely fabulous experience at a small, relatively unknown company yet find it difficult to convince another company to hire you. This is often the case with people who attempt to make the move from a small company to a large one. Many large companies tend to have tunnel vision in this respect because they question whether someone from a smaller company could handle the work without being eaten alive. This is especially true if the other company is so small that most people haven't heard of it. The comparison is not always fair, but the perception is definitely something to keep in mind.

My point is not to bash small companies. Far from it. Small companies can be wonderful because they often provide more access to top management and more direct involvement in the day-to-day business. But be aware that the career path from a large company to a small one is far easier than the other way around. That's not to say, however, that it can't be done. It definitely can. It's often just a tougher sell because it requires job hunters to sell themselves based on their experience and actual contributions rather than the reputation of the company. Some companies are so anxious to attract

> Few people do business well who do nothing else. —*Earl of Chesterfield*

employees who have worked for larger, established companies that they don't always screen as well as they should. While this makes it easier for the job hunter, it doesn't necessarily do either party any favors, because both parties miss an opportunity to learn as much about each other as they otherwise might.

It should be noted that large companies are often valued for their superior benefits packages, but this is not the most important factor to consider. Whether you are challenged, stimulated, and developing personally and professionally is more important. If that isn't happening, no amount of life insurance, health insurance, or profit sharing will bring you the happiness you deserve.

Reputation of a company

If you must rely on the trade press to assess a company's reputation, use more than one article and publication. This will balance the impact of writers who might be less than objective. In any case, start by comparing the facts. For each potential employer, make a list of the clients they serve, the product categories they sell, and the services they provide.

From a job-hunting perspective, the Internet is the very best resource for research. Though it would be a mistake to make it the sole tool in your arsenal, there is no better way to access information on a company and its competition.

Let's imagine that Dell Computer Corporation is on your list. It isn't necessary to list or memorize every product Dell carries. There are too many variations. Instead, go to their website (dell.com) and familiarize yourself with the different product categories, such as desktop computers, laptops, and servers.

Next, read the press reports or news stories. If the company doesn't have a link to news items, go to a website that specializes in news. For example, if the company is publicly traded, go to one of the financial websites. By typing in the company name or ticker symbol, you can get recent news items, analyst reports, stock prices, and charts. Some of the better websites include (in alphabetical order):

- cnn.com
- moneycentral.com
- msnbc.com
- nasdaq.com
- pcquote.com

For publicly traded companies, it's also helpful to read quarterly and annual reports (known as 10Q and 10K reports, respectively). In the not so distant past, people had to pay big bucks to get access to this information. Now, it's available for a small fee from Edgar-Online: www.edgar-online.com.

Next, you will want to determine the company's vision for long-term growth and profitability. If you can find the annual or quarterly reports, as you would for any publicly traded company, take the time to read the section entitled "Management Discussion & Analysis." This can be an interesting source of information about the business environment, opportunities, and challenges the company is currently facing. Look specifically for clues about what will fuel future growth.

You may even find some information the company would probably rather not have disclosed. For example, you might learn that five major customers account for 72 percent of the company's total sales. Should you decide to interview at the company, a legitimate question to ask would be, "Given that a relatively small number of customers represent over 70 percent of your sales, what steps have been taken to ensure the company's long-term financial stability should one or more of those customers switch to a competitor?"

Whatever the company's strategy, you want some assurance that the exodus of a large client won't necessarily result in massive layoffs. Job hunting can be fun, but it isn't so much fun that you'd want to be back on the street a few months after finding what you thought was the perfect job. Another great website as you gather independent research is Hoover's. You can find this site at www.hoovers.com.

Yahoo! and other websites even carry inside trading information for publicly traded companies. With a few clicks of the mouse you can find out which executives bought or sold stock in their own company, how many shares they traded, and how much they paid or received. In short, there isn't much you can't find out if you know where to look.

If the company you're researching doesn't happen to be publicly traded, you have a few good options in gathering information. Start with the news services and pay particular attention to local papers in the city where the company headquarters is located. For example, McDonald's corporate headquarters is in Oakbrook, Illinois, so the *Chicago Tribune* and the *Chicago Sun-Times* would be more inclined to cover company news, since many of the subscribers are either McDonald's employees or people who have friends and relatives who work for the company. In some cases, when you use the Internet and access the archives of major newspapers, you may be charged for downloading the entire article. The investment is probably well worth it, unless you already have free access to a system like Lexis/Nexis, a popular legal and news service that provides the entire text of every article from newspapers around the country. While Lexis/Nexis is prohibitively expensive for the average person, you may be able to access it through your college or university. If you don't have access, there are other easy ways to access the information free of charge. Steve Waterhouse, a professional speaker and tireless researcher of companies, considers the following Internet sites the best news sources around:

- ajr.org (American Journalism Review/AJR News Link)
- avantgo.com (Avantgo)
- bizjournals.com (Biz Journals)
- infobeat.com (InfoBeat)

The AJR News Link is a particularly useful resource because it provides a link to every major newspaper in the country. Biz Journals is another wonderful source because it includes a powerful feature called "SearchWatch," that allows you to type in keywords such as companies or names. Biz Journals will then notify you by E-mail when articles are published that include your search terms. This is a great way to keep up on the news that most interests you.

Another great way to research large private companies is through the industry reports published by major brokerage firms like PaineWebber, William Blair, and Goldman Sachs. If the company is a major player and competes with publicly traded companies, chances are excellent that it will be included in the report. To get these reports, find someone who works at a brokerage firm who would be willing to help you track down the research.

First, call the brokerage firm and ask for the research department. Once you get through, ask if the firm has an analyst who covers whatever industry you happen to be researching. If the company doesn't, contact other firms until you find one that does. Then, ask for a copy of the analyst's reports. This may not work if you don't have an account at the firm, in which case you'll need to be creative. For example, you might start by calling recent graduates of your college or university who are employed by brokerage firms.

If you're having trouble finding an analyst who covers a particular industry, call the investor relations department at one of the large publicly traded companies in the industry and ask for help. Tell the representative you're doing research on the industry and need specific information about some of the company's private competitors. The investor relations people may have some valuable suggestions. At the very least, they'll be able to tell you what brokerage firms have analysts who cover the industry because it's their job to set up conference calls with analysts.

As you read through the reports of industry analysts, pay particular attention to the growth rate for the company as well as the industry. Growing companies in growing industries are ideal. Analyst reports can also be a great place to learn how well particular companies are positioned within the industry. You might even find ideas for similar companies to target in your job search.

Some of the information above can also be accessed through the trade press and company promotional literature. The trade press is a good source for industry news, marketing trends, salary surveys, and other general information. If you have trouble locating specific information, ask the reference librarian at your local library.

For information on employee attrition, you may have to dig a little deeper, but it's worth the effort if you have concerns about employee morale. If you know someone at the company, that would be the best place to start. This may require high levels of diplomacy on your part. For example, you might ask if most employees tend to stay with the company for years or if there is a fair amount of turnover.

If you don't know anyone at the company, use this as an opportunity to build a relationship with a headhunter who specializes in the industry. Although we'll discuss the pros and cons of working with headhunters in more detail later, this is one area where they can add significant value to your research efforts. As specialists in an industry, headhunters have daily contact with people at all levels, which often gives them firsthand knowledge about morale, salary structures, and other issues of importance.

To learn more about employee satisfaction, you might also check out The Job Vault at vaultreports.com. This site provides employer profiles for large public and private companies as well as large nonprofit organizations. The Job Vault also rates companies based on employee opinions across categories like job satisfaction, pay, and dress code.

Nonprofit companies

If you're researching nonprofit companies, you'll need a completely different strategy because brokerage firms and financial websites aren't likely to have much information. In this case, you will want to visit the following websites specializing in nonprofits:

- idealist.org (Idealist offers information on over 23,000 nonprofit organizations.)
- pnnonline.org (Philanthropy News Network provides information about nonprofits and foundations as well as links to many of the sites.)

Using the Internet to Market Yourself

To make life as easy as possible, put your résumé together using a program like Microsoft Word or WordPerfect. That way, you can send the file as an E-mail attachment and be relatively sure anyone can download it without difficulty. To date, I have received hundreds if not thousands of résumés via E-mail. With these popular word-processing programs, any problems or formatting issues will be relatively minor. In contrast, when people create résumés using other programs, it becomes a hit or miss proposition whether the average person will be able to download it. Whatever you do, don't paste the résumé in the body of an E-mail message. Almost without exception, this formatting is so horrendous, anyone would dread the thought of reading it.

To avoid these issues, send yourself the résumé via E-mail to see how it looks. You might even consider setting up a separate E-mail account at hotmail.com or one of the other free services to use exclusively for your job search. That way, you can also use it to test how well attachments are transmitted.

On some websites, you can't just upload your résumé as is. Instead, you have to input the data using a website-dictated format. If this is the case, use it as an opportunity to reexamine every word to make sure it contributes to the overall selling message. Unfortunately, this ignores the possibility that you might need to reposition the résumé for particular job opportunities. As a result, you may be forced to post a more general résumé. This is just one of the short-comings of on-line job hunting. Of course, this also raises the question of whether posting a résumé online is a good idea in the first place. My answer is, once again: it depends.

If you are currently employed and the company doesn't know that you're looking, posting a résumé is not terribly discreet. Just as it is possible to do a keyword search for skills, it is equally possible to do a keyword search for company or individual names. I know because I used to do it all the time. Using this method, it would only take an employer a few seconds to search even the largest database for the résumés of current employees. That's not long for your secret to get out.

I've also come across electronic résumés in which the candidate's name and past employers were disguised. For example, rather than list the company name, it would say "$75 billion pharmaceutical company" or "$745 million computer network equipment manufacturer." Although I still don't recommend that you post your résumé on the Internet while you're currently employed, this is definitely a more discreet way to do it.

Just as you should be cautious when responding to blind newspaper ads, you should show caution on the Internet. When I worked at the search firm, we often placed general ads on job search websites without revealing the name of our client. We didn't include the name because people might then have gone directly to the company. Our clients didn't want that to happen. That's why they were paying us to handle the search. Anyway, we often received résumés from people who were already at the company and looking to get out. Needless to say, these people would have been horrified had they known how close they came to sending their own company a résumé and cover letter talking about how anxious they were leave.

Working directly with a headhunter and networking on your own can help you avoid these career-threatening pitfalls.

Job search websites

If you're not currently employed or you're about to be laid off and being discreet is not your chief concern, then go ahead and post your résumé on-line. From what I've seen, there are only three general websites I would recommend: monster.com, headhunter.net, and employmentspot.com. The first two have a user-friendly format to guide you through the process of adding your résumé to the database. At that point, potential employers and executive recruiters alike will be able to access your résumé by searching for keywords.

The third is perhaps the best place to start your online search. Employmentspot.com is the Yahoo! of career websites. It is a portal that keeps track of job search websites and provides links. Better still, the site divides this huge category into manageable chunks by location and vocation. It even provides links for executive, entry-level, part-time, seasonal, volunteer, freelance, internship, and minority job hunters. Definitely a worthwhile site—especially if you are in the beginning stages of your search.

> I have always been naively guided by the principle that if we do not believe in the products we advertise strongly enough to use them ourselves, or at least to give them a real try, we are not completely honest with ourselves in advertising them to others. The very least we can do is to remain neutral.　—*Leo Burnett*

> The price one pays for pursuing any profession or calling is an intimate knowledge of its ugly side.
> —*James Baldwin*

Every industry has specific words or phrases associated with it, and these same words are the ones a company's representatives are likely to use as they search for candidates. With this in mind, you can put together a résumé that will show up during these keyword searches. Just make sure you have the experience to back it up. Depending on your experience, it may be worthwhile to include a separate category on your résumé listing the skills you've developed that might be the subject of a search. However you structure it, make it compelling. Getting your résumé to come up on a search and getting people to call you are two completely different issues.

Closely monitoring the job postings on industry-specific websites is often more effective than posting your résumé. For example, when we were doing a search for

an Internet marketing person, we posted ads on headhunter.net, monster.com, and the Direct Marketing Association websites. In the end, however, we found the ideal candidate through our posting on the Chicago Interactive Marketing Association website.

If you use this approach, check the website regularly for updates. The best jobs don't remain open forever.

Clients, Products, or Services

Before you accept a job with any company, it's important to remember that you will be a representative of the company—no matter what your job title. To the outside world, everyone who works for the company represents the company. In much the same way, the corporate values and standards also reflect on you. For example, it's important to remember that almost all of a company's income comes from the sale of its products and, more indirectly, from client products. This can have a profound impact on your overall career satisfaction and happiness should you suddenly realize that you have issues with your company, clients, or the industry in general.

For example, when I worked as a headhunter, our company specialized in direct marketing. Over time, the whole concept of junk mail began to bother me from an environmental standpoint. While there are many companies within the direct marketing industry who wouldn't be considered tradi-

in an industry that promotes the manufacturing, distribution, and advertising of controversial items. Would you have any difficulty promoting or representing beer, wine, liquor, condoms, cigarettes, sports cars, or defense contractors? I'm not suggesting that you, as an employee of a company, dedicate your life to smoking, drinking, or anything else you find objectionable. However, if you're employed in a particular industry, you should support the responsible promotion and distribution of its products.

tional junk mail companies, I often struggled with the fact that the industry as a whole had probably done more to damage the environment (by chopping down trees for mailings that end up in the garbage) than almost any other industry except perhaps the chemical industry. Even though our company never sent direct mailings, we were often paid by companies that did. To me, that felt just as bad.

In a service business, such as advertising, most of an agency's revenue comes from the sale of its clients' products. For this reason it makes sense to find a company with products and clients you would be proud to represent. In his book *Ogilvy on Advertising*, David Ogilvy describes going to great lengths to support client products. Ogilvy, who was known for his impeccable appearance, stocked his wardrobe with suits from Sears Roebuck—a longtime client.

The issue of supporting client products is especially important if you hope to work

Creating Other Opportunities

As you evaluate career options, look beyond the obvious industry-specific opportunities. Too many people assume they are pigeonholed into a particular career based on their areas of study, and never realize they can transfer their skills to related opportunities. Take the time to think, in broad terms, about the skills you have developed. Then challenge yourself to put together a list of different groups of people who might value those skills. For example, if you are a person who enjoys research and writing, you could certainly contact market research companies. But you could also contact university professors who need help collecting and compiling research to include in their books.

If you are of an entrepreneurial inclination, you might gain experience helping small local businesses in your field of interest. This is especially applicable to anyone interested in marketing. Unlike doctors and lawyers, marketers do not need a license or an advanced degree to practice. You don't even need original ideas. The desire and ability to execute business-building programs is enough.

Selling by listening

Before contacting anyone, take the time to understand the business, the consumer, the competition, and the market opportunity. Then write a letter of introduction describing what you have to offer and why it is valuable. A letter is better than a phone call or personal visit because it shows more effort. Anyone can make a phone call. Not everyone can write a convincing letter.

This strategy can work anywhere. If you haven't graduated from college, you might even use it to find a summer job. If you come up empty-handed, remember to give yourself credit for the effort. When you do finally succeed, you will have the extra sense of accomplishment that only comes from creating something from nothing.

Once you have arranged a meeting with a business owner, you'll probably be anxious to share your ideas. Enthusiasm is important. Listening is even more important. One of my first meetings as a freelance consultant was with the CEO of a development-stage software company. Once we shook hands, he opened the conversation saying, "I have no particular agenda." He proceeded to spend the next thirty minutes describing his hopes, dreams, and visions. At that

point, selling myself was easy because I knew exactly what he needed. Since I'd been brought in to rewrite the company's business plan, I was able to compare what the CEO told me with what I already knew from reading the existing plan. As it turned out, none of the enthusiasm or opportunity came across in the plan. By taking notes and creating a list of ideas that occurred to me as he spoke, I was able to highlight what was missing and share my ideas for improving it. There is no substitute for active listening.

Building a Network

Getting a job in any field is a matter of hard work, homework, and dedication. For many, the hardest part of the job search is building a strong network. Nevertheless, the only way to impress the right people is to meet them. This may sound basic, but my experience suggests that people are reluctant to seek assistance—particularly when strangers are involved.

For example, not long after I graduated from Northwestern, some friends and I organized an informational meeting to share what we learned about the recruiting process. About fifty graduate students attended. At the end of the evening, I extended an open invitation to anyone who wanted help in the job search. Secretly, I feared there would be more requests than I could handle.

My fears weren't even partially realized. I received one call the next day, and even that person didn't follow through. Several months later I was surprised to hear

The Hard Work of Being in the Right Place at the Right Time

Jim Floyd is one of those rare individuals who seems to have found the perfect job. Anyone meeting him for the first time would be struck by his peaceful, easygoing nature and genuine connectedness with friends and strangers alike. However, what makes Jim even more exceptional is what he went through to become the person he is today.

As his high school classmates wrote college applications, Jim found himself thinking more about singing, acting, and a career on the stage. Although Jim's family respected his talents, they were concerned when he decided to skip college. In his parents' opinion, Jim wasn't taking a risk, he was making a mistake. They didn't see how his passion or ability could overcome a lack of experience, an absence of formal training, or the intense competition. Nevertheless, Jim trusted his instincts and focused on his goal.

After graduation, Jim put his heart and voice into auditions. Through persistence, he earned the lead role in a production that eventually toured the country. For the next few years life was better than he'd ever imagined.

During his third season with the touring company, Jim lost his voice in the middle of a performance. Unable to speak and deeply concerned, Jim sought the help of a throat specialist. A thorough examination confirmed the worst. Jim's vocal chords showed signs of prolonged strain and abuse. His speaking voice would eventually return, but the damage was permanent. He would never sing again. His career was over.

Knowing that the condition was preventable made the circumstances even harder to accept. Had Jim taken voice lessons, he could have acquired the skills that would have preserved his career by minimizing the daily damage to his vocal chords. Unfortunately, the natural power and character of Jim's voice camouflaged his underlying need for instruction.

With little more than a high school education and the vague desire to remain in the entertainment industry, Jim began his search for a new career. When family considerations made it necessary to return to Pennsylvania, Jim was forced to add a geographical constraint to his expanding list of obstacles. Fortunately, his spirit remained intact. Rather than focus on his problems, he set new goals and pursued them relentlessly.

continued

Before moving from Nashville to Pennsylvania, Jim contacted a headhunter and explained his situation. Although the prospect didn't thrill him, he even expressed a willingness to commute to New York or New Jersey if necessary. According to the headhunter, a publication identified only as *Radio/TV Interview Reports* was conducting a nationwide search for someone to act as a liaison between television producers and talk show guests. Interested applicants were given the following instructions:

We don't care about your résumé. We are more interested in how you come across on the phone. Call the toll-free number. Leave a message. Tell us why we should hire you. If we like what we hear, we'll call you back.

For Jim, this wasn't enough. He picked up the phone, but he didn't call the 800 number. Instead, he called directory assistance to find out who owned the number. The phone company wouldn't reveal the customer's name, but it did tell him where the calls were directed. To his delight, the town was in Pennsylvania.

With the help of a local phone book, Jim compiled a list of companies that could have placed the ad. A few phone calls later, Jim discovered that the publisher of *Radio/TV Interview Reports* was a company named Bradley Communications. By learning as much as he could about the company and the publication, Jim began to understand the company's needs. Having spent so much time in the entertainment industry, he was particularly well-acquainted with television producers. That, combined with his extensive experience on stage, made him a natural to act as a liaison between talk show producers and the experts, authorities, and celebrities they brought on as guests. Armed with this information, Jim bypassed the 800 number and sent a letter directly to Bradley's president.

By the end of the search, Bradley Communications had received messages from 1,200 interested applicants. Although many offered more in the way of education and experience, none could match Jim for enthusiasm and potential. Jim was the only person who took the time to identify the company and understand its business. Not surprisingly, he got the job.

Using a phone book and other common resources, Jim demonstrated resourcefulness, persistence, and a desire to contribute to the company. To smart companies, these qualities are far more valuable than college degrees, related experiences, and other artificial measures of potential.

that most of the students were still unemployed. As graduation neared, they were shifting into panic mode. Yet they still didn't call. The situation described above is sadly typical. The people who worry most about the future are also least likely to take steps to shape it. If the industry professionals I know are any indication, the reluctance to pursue job contacts and informational interviews is widespread. The remedy, however, is simple.

Ask for help before you ask for a job

This is the job-hunting equivalent of the "foot in the door" technique used in sales. By honestly seeking the advice of a potential employer, you can get a person to lower his or her natural defenses. First, use the career counseling office at your school and an alumni directory to identify contacts. Once you have found several contacts, write a brief note describing who you are, what you hope to accomplish, and how they can help. If the person is already in the industry, take the time to prepare a résumé that clearly addresses the needs of his or her company. With this as a starting point, you will be better able to create a high impact presentation.

Finally, request an informational interview. Then follow up with a phone call. Even if the person doesn't have any helpful ideas, you have lost nothing. On the other hand, he or she may put you in touch with someone at another company or division. It happens all the time.

Trade press/industry experts

Industry-specific magazines can be wonderful resources for job hunters. Some even offer regional editions. Find a few that you like and read them faithfully. When you read a relevant or interesting article, contact executives who were quoted. In doing so, make it clear that you value their time and are worthy of their assistance.

One particularly resourceful friend of mine, Andy, made some of his best contacts by writing to people who had recently been quoted or interviewed in such a magazine. Almost without exception, he received a warm response because people were thrilled to receive the attention. Andy appealed to their egos, and they rewarded him with their time.

This tactic does not have to be limited to job hunting. I have used this technique to secure expert advice on a variety of topics, and it hasn't failed yet. Further, I haven't found any correlation between a person's professional or social prominence and their willingness to help. One highly regarded expert returned my call and agreed to review a business plan I was writing. He didn't charge me for his time or expert opinion because he shared my enthusiasm for the subject and just wanted to help.

University alumni

If the job search takes you to an unfamiliar city, contact alumni in the area. The people you call don't have to be in the same industry. Just send a note and introduce yourself as a recent graduate of their alma mater. Mention that you just moved to the area and ask for ideas, advice, or professional contacts. As always, prepare specific questions.

You might wonder why an alum would take time to help a total stranger who isn't even interested in the same field. It doesn't make sense until you sit on the other side of the desk. People who agree to serve as alumni contacts for their school do so because they genuinely want to help—even if it's only to put you in touch with someone in your field. They remember what it's like to be in your shoes, and they didn't like it any better than you do. Nevertheless, most alumni don't get the opportunity to help because relatively few people ever use this valuable resource. It's unfortunate how few job-hunting candidates are willing to take a chance like this, because this approach communicates courage, confidence, and resourcefulness more convincingly than a résumé ever could. Taking this step may be daunting, but I assure you it's worth the effort.

Advertising

Help wanted ads In general, job listings are not a good place to find attractive leads. To minimize training and administrative costs, as well as the risk associated with hiring an unknown commodity, a company will often hire from within. When that isn't possible, the company can use word-of-mouth to explore the wider professional community.

For companies using the approach described above, the expense of reaching a broader, less-qualified audience through job listings is less efficient. It is also more expensive, not only because of the advertising cost, but also because a large response will increase the amount of time recruiters spend screening unqualified candidates.

Through the process described above, the most attractive jobs are filled long before a classified ad would be considered. From an applicant's point of view, relying upon help wanted ads has a number of serious shortcomings. First, if the ad is effective, the number of people who respond can be quite high—i.e., the better the ad, the greater the competition (quantity not quality). Second, the best jobs rarely make the job listings.

Reverse ads If you have a particular skill or interest and have no practical way to narrow your target audience of potential companies, you might consider placing an ad briefly describing your skills and how they would be valuable to a company. Should you pursue this strategy, take the time to craft your ad to be benefit-oriented. The company should know exactly what you have to offer and why what you offer would be helpful.

If the first ad fails to generate interest, revise or rewrite it and run it again. For example, if the first ad described the position you sought, start the second ad with a question that addresses the problem you'd solve. If you specialize in organizing personal and work space, you might ask, "Have you ever lost time searching for a misplaced memo?" Once you have the reader's attention, it will be easier to get him or her to respond. But remember, copywriting is an art. It may take a few revisions to get the response you desire.

Since this is a technique relatively few people think to use, there is no standard approach. Likewise, the response rates will differ from one publication to the next. Nevertheless, there are two strategic issues to address. First, you must decide what magazine, newspaper, or newsletter would be the most appropriate vehicle. For example, if you have an area of specialization such as industrial engineering, it would make more sense to run the ad in a trade publication that caters to industrial engineers than to run it in your local general interest paper; depending on the overall circulation, it might also be cheaper. Next, you have to determine where to place the ad within a particular publication. Here again there are no rules of thumb. Instead, I recommend consulting with the classified sales people at the publication because they probably know the audience better than anyone else. From their own day-to-day contact with readers they know what people expect to see and where they go to find specific information. If the first person you talk to doesn't inspire confidence, call back later and talk to someone else. You might also ask to talk with a supervisor or advertising manager. With the optimal placement, the ad can work harder

for you and you'll feel better about making the investment.

Anonymous ads Responding to an anonymous ad might not seem like an issue, but it is. From a strategic standpoint, this approach makes almost no sense because you cannot position yourself for a job and a company you know nothing about. I would advise that you not waste your time using this approach in your job search.

The risk is substantially higher for people who are currently employed because their own company may have placed the ad. This faux pas would have the same impact on a person's job security as sending the boss an E-mail that read:

My heart's not in my work right now.
If you can't reach me, I'm probably out
looking for another job.

Headhunters and Recruiters

Before we move on to the specifics of how to market yourself and your skills effectively, it's important to explore some of the other resources that may make your job search easier. Although this might come as a surprise, headhunters and executive recruiters can be valuable resources even for entry-level candidates and career changers. However, it's up to you to find the right headhunters. You can't wait for them to find you.

One of the best resources for identifying the right headhunters is *The Directory of Executive Recruiters*. This reference guide, available in most libraries, divides search firms by specialty, location, and whether they work on a contingency or retained basis. Most search firms tend to specialize in a particular area such as high-tech, finance, legal, engineering, direct marketing, advertising, or secretarial. Within each specialty, there may also be companies that focus on president or executive-level, middle management, or junior-level searches. Using this directory, you should be able to put together a comprehensive list of firms to contact.

While you could add this information to your job search journal, you'd be better off investing in a contact management system like Maximizer, produced by Multiactive Software. Maximizer will allow you to keep track of all the people you've written to, spoken with, or interviewed with during the course of your job search. For the most part, I don't like to endorse particular products, but this program is especially good because it is extremely easy to use and you can tailor it to your exact specifications. It's also very affordable, as software programs go. For more information, check out the Multiactive website at maximizer.com.

Once you've decided on a particular industry, take the time to introduce yourself to as many recruiters as you can—even at firms that specialize in executive placements. While an executive search firm would probably never be retained exclusively to find entry-level candidates, they may be hired to do so in conjunction with

another search. Also, some search firms help entry-level candidates by presenting them at no charge to existing clients. This builds goodwill among clients and candidates alike. Besides, today's entry-level candidates will be tomorrow's executives.

At the hands of a headhunter

Even after I started working full-time, it never occurred to me to contact a headhunter—otherwise known as an executive recruiter. At the time, I was thrilled with my job and couldn't imagine working anywhere else. Even if that had not been the case, I naively thought headhunters only called people when they knew something about their reputation and ability.

Now, after having worked as a headhunter myself for several years, I understand and appreciate what a valuable resource headhunters can be—even for entry-level candidates and career changers. However, for this strategy to be most effective, it's important to take your time aligning yourself with appropriate executive search firms because not all headhunters are created equal.

Contingency versus retained search

First, you, the candidate, should never be charged for the services of a recruiter, and you should avoid any employment service that promises you a job and either charges

pleting even the most difficult assignments. Otherwise, companies would never be willing to pay these recruiters up front. By working on a retained basis, these search firms have the luxury of working with a short, select list of clients. Contingency firms, on the other hand, have to work with a much broader range of clients to increase their chances of making a placement.

Contingency recruiting The pressure contingency recruiters face to generate income is, unfortunately, what leads some to questionable business practices. For example, some contingency recruiters treat the business as a numbers game and routinely present résumés without the permission of the candidates. This is both indiscreet and unprofessional. If you decide to submit your paperwork to a contingency firm, emphasize that representatives are not to present you or your credentials without permission.

Another downside to working with a contingency recruiter is that representatives may talk with you about an intriguing position, but they won't always tell you the name of the company. Contingency firms do this to protect themselves from candidates who might contact the company on their own before the recruiter has a chance to present them. Other candidates, who work with multiple search firms, might let another recruiter present them for the same opportunity. Either way, the contingency firm's fee is in jeopardy.

Contingency recruiters frequently compete against other contingency recruiters. As such, filling an open position becomes a

you a fee up front or expects you to pay a percentage of your first year's salary. To be blunt, these firms prey on gullible, desperate job hunters. Having eliminated these charlatans from your consideration, there are only two types of recruiters remaining: contingency firms and retained firms.

At the most basic level, the distinction between contingency recruiters and retained search firms concerns how they are compensated. Contingency firms make money only when one of their candidates is placed. Retained firms, on the other hand, are paid a fee in advance by the hiring company. Considering that the hiring company pays the fee in both cases, you may be wondering why the distinction is important from the candidate's viewpoint.

As it happens, the way recruiters are compensated directly impacts their professional practices. Ideally, this shouldn't be the case, but unfortunately it is. Generally speaking, retained search firms have both an area of specialization and a strong network of contacts. Through years of focus within a particular industry, retained search firms tend to build a high level of credibility and a reputation for successfully com-race against the clock. For this reason, some contingency firms take shortcuts by presenting candidates they have never interviewed.

Retained searches When a retained firm accepts an assignment and takes a fee in advance, it is responsible for completing the search, no matter how long it takes. However, since retained recruiters aren't racing against the clock, they have the luxury of being able to talk in depth with candidates, hiring managers, and others at the hiring company. Further, since they don't have to worry about losing their fee to another recruiter, retained firms can tell potential candidates everything they know, including the name of the company.

To protect their reputation and make sure a candidate is worth presenting, retained search firms do extensive interviews and reference checks. Whereas contingency recruiters tend to submit as many candidates as possible, retained firms, focus more on quality. When I worked in retained search, there were a number of positions we filled after having presented a single candidate. This, however, only happens when there is a truly strong match between the client's needs and the candidate's skills.

From a candidate's perspective, the only real downside to retained recruiters is that they work with fewer clients. Therefore, at any given time they may or may not have an assignment that fits your interests or background. With a good contingency firm your odds of finding out about an appropriate position may be slightly better.

Tips for working with headhunters

Letters of introduction Once you have identified headhunters who specialize in your industry, send a résumé and a letter of introduction. A letter of introduction differs from a cover letter because it describes, in detail, the type of position you seek without focusing on a particular company. In the letter, be sure to include whether you'd be willing to relocate and your salary history—even if you were undercompensated in your previous positions. This is important because it will help ensure that the recruiters don't waste your time presenting you with opportunities that are too far out of range in either direction. Sharing your salary history is also important because the headhunter handles all offers and negotiations. From a candidate's perspective, this can be a huge blessing.

Be specific about your goals One of the biggest mistakes people make in working with headhunters is being too vague about their goals. The only way headhunters will remember you when the right opportunity comes along is if they associate you with a particular job description. In contrast, if you aren't specific about what you want, they won't remember you at all.

If you're changing careers, focusing on a particular path is even more important because it will make it easier to convince people that you've done your homework and know what you want.

Working with more than one firm You owe it to yourself to make yourself known to as many reputable firms as you wish. But first take the time to build a relationship with a particular recruiter at each firm, even if it's by phone.

If you're working with more than one firm, it's your responsibility to manage the process. Under no circumstances should you let more than one firm present you to the same hiring company. I've seen that happen on several occasions, and it makes everyone look bad—especially the candidate. Some companies will reject a candidate outright if they receive the paperwork from more than one recruiter. This happens for two reasons. First, the company may not want to get into an argument over which recruiter gets credit for the placement. At the same time, the company may question the candidate's poor judgment and apparent inability to manage the process. For some companies, this raises enough of a question that they will simply eliminate the candidate. Don't let this happen to you.

Be honest about your past Headhunters can deal with anything as long as they know the truth. If you've been fired from a previous job, be honest about that. You aren't the first person this has happened to, and you won't be the last. Be candid about what happened, but more important, describe what you learned from the experience. I have much more respect for people who face the reality of their past than try to hide it. Besides, the world is too small for secrets like that. If you don't face it now, the truth will look a lot uglier when it is eventually discovered.

Follow up and stay in touch As much as I wish every candidate was top-of-mind all the time, or at least at the right times, it's simply not possible. To give you some additional perspective, consider this: during the two years I worked full time as a headhunter, I had contact with over 2,500 candidates. Knowing that I couldn't possibly call everyone with a weekly or monthly update, I encouraged people to call me. Don't be shy. The only way you will be top-of-mind at the right time is if you call and check in on a regular basis. Even after you get a job, stay in touch. One of the worst feelings as a recruiter is coming across the perfect job for a candidate and not being able to find him or her.

Now that we've covered the basic resources that exist for identifying opportunities, it's time to look within to find the reasons potential employers would be thrilled to have you on the team. This will prove to be the most important and illuminating step in the entire process. Unfortunately, it's also the step people are most likely to miss.

The Self-Assessment

Although countless pages have been written about job hunting, much of the information is hopelessly inadequate. Read enough on the subject and you might think appearance counts for more than presentation. It doesn't.

The key to a successful job search is effective preparation. This includes, but is not limited to, collecting as much information as possible about the industry, the company, and the position. In addition, much of your time should be spent matching your qualifications with the company's expectations. In other words, give the company specific reasons to hire you. You have something to offer. Tell them what it is.

It often happens that the best marketing opportunities involve positioning a product for a niche market. Likewise, the way you define and redefine yourself can play a role

> Keep growing, silently and earnestly through your whole development; you couldn't disturb it any more violently than by looking outside and waiting for outside answers to questions that only your innermost feeling, in your quietest hour, can perhaps answer.
>
> —*Rainer Maria Rilke,* Letters to a Young Poet

in your job search. What interests or experiences enhance your professional value? For example, are you fluent in a foreign language? It amazes me how few people are willing to leverage their foreign language abilities. Even people who have lived a year or more in another culture and are able to carry on a conversation in another language are sometimes hesitant to list the skill on their résumé. The fact is, you do not have to speak and write with the comfort level of a native to be considered fluent. And you don't have to be completely fluent for the skill to be of value to a potential employer. More often than not, even people who have immersed themselves in another culture are unwilling to list the experience on their résumé. It's as if people have an overwhelming insecurity that their ability to speak and write in a foreign language must be absolutely flawless to be worth mentioning. It doesn't. If you feel the need to qualify your language ability with words like "passable" or "proficient," go ahead. Like-

wise, if you speak fluently but aren't proficient as a writer, list speaking and writing separately with the appropriate qualifiers. For example: Japanese (speaking: fluent, writing: limited).

Don't ignore this valuable skill. Even a limited ability may be enough for you to be considered for interesting overseas projects that would otherwise never have been an option.

Valuable life experiences and marketable skills are not limited to language ability. Take time to reflect on every aspect of your life and how it differs from what others experience. Don't take anything for granted. For example, if you were raised by an interracial couple or homosexual parents, you're probably more sensitive to the feelings and needs of people from different backgrounds. While this may not be what people traditionally think of as a marketable skill, the experience could be a valuable selling point if you're applying for a job that requires heightened sensitivity to a diverse group of people, clients, or customers. For these reasons, uncovering the skills, abilities, and experiences that set you apart is an important step in marketing yourself effectively.

If you are fortunate to have a particularly interesting or unusual background, consider what types of companies or organizations would value your experience. The experience doesn't have to be exotic. If you grew up on a farm and earned an MBA, you might highlight the discipline and independence you gained from farming. In addition, your knowledge of farming combined with your business education would probably be invaluable to agricultural companies and the marketing firms that represent them. Not everyone can get an MBA. Not everyone grows up on a farm. Fewer still do both.

Do you know yourself?

It seems like you should already be an expert in this area. Nevertheless, this is where most candidates fall apart. A few well-chosen questions by an interviewer can easily demonstrate inadequate preparation. To be unconvincing and unprepared to deal with questions about who you are and why you want to work in a particular industry is no different than sending yourself a rejection letter on the corporate letterhead of your choice.

I cannot stress enough how important preparation is. You'll need to think about every aspect of your life in order to be ready to face an interviewer. A complete and thoughtful self-analysis is the first step in creating your personal marketing plan. While you may never be asked every question on the following pages, each, in its own way, will help you understand the person you are today.

Before you get started, I strongly recommend buying a hardcover journal for your self-analysis. A journal is better than a spiral-bound notebook because it will last longer. This way, when you decide to change jobs or careers, a lot of the initial soul searching will already be done. The journal will also make a nice keepsake to remind you of experiences, thoughts, and feelings you might otherwise have forgotten.

Use the questions that follow to stimulate your thinking. Take detailed notes. Know exactly who you are, what you like, what you want to do, and why you want to do it.

To help guide you in the process, I have elaborated on each question and its importance to the job search process. Where appropriate, I've also indicated the questions you may encounter in an interview. While questions about age, race, ethnicity, religion, sexual preference, and marital status cannot legally be asked in an interview, these factors may play an important role in defining who you are. As such, they are important to consider during the self-analysis.

Questions for Self-Analysis

Family/growing up

What role did you play in your family?

Are you the youngest? Oldest? Somewhere in the middle? Did parental illnesses or issues result in you taking on adult responsibility at an early age? In chronological time, you may only be twenty-two years old, but you may have the maturity of someone much older. Considering the number of recent college graduates who lack maturity, this can be a real selling point.

This isn't necessarily a question that will come up in an interview, but it can be important in understanding the impact your family has had on the person you are today.

When conflicts arose in your family, how did you handle it?

Are you a peacemaker or negotiator? Or are you a mischievous troublemaker at heart? Believe it or not, this can play a role in your career path. For example, some family peacemakers find that they have dealt with enough personality conflicts to realize they have no interest in managing or being responsible for people. They would rather work independently. Others thrive on their skill as negotiators and managers. It truly depends on the person. Just know your truth, whatever it is. Here again, this question is not likely to come up in an interview. Nevertheless, it can provide great insight into preferences that ultimately impact your choice of working environment.

How has the marital status of your parents impacted the person you have become?

Are your parents best friends who have been ideal role models of love, patience, and forgiveness? If so, you are truly blessed. Unfortunately, this has become more rare. In any event, the marital status of your parents is not nearly as important as what you learned from the situation. If your parents were not great communicators, you might be more committed to dealing with everyone honestly and openly. On the other hand, if you never learned to share your feelings, you might harbor some serious hostility. Like it or not, many of these same issues will arise again and again in the working world. The disagreements may be different, but the dynamics and the feelings will often be the same.

Did you grow up in one place or did you move often?

The degree of stability, or instability, you had growing up does not automatically impact you one way or another. Like every other issue, it becomes a question of how you played the cards you were dealt. Some children who move frequently are outgoing and confident enough to establish solid friendships wherever they go. Others, who are more sensitive to the pain of leaving friends, may become more withdrawn. Even within the same family you can see children who have different reactions to the same situation. Although reactions will vary, it's a good exercise for determining preferences.

From a career perspective, this question is important because you will be more comfortable if you pursue jobs in keeping with your tolerance for risk and change. If you crave stability and avoid uncertainty, there are certain entrepreneurial career paths that would terrify you. Likewise, if you find excitement in uncertainty, you would do well to avoid the monotony of traditional desk jobs.

If you could relive one day from your childhood, which one would it be? Why?

From a purely psychological standpoint, this is an interesting question because it can bring a wide range of feelings to the surface. People who set extraordinarily high standards for themselves may hear this question and immediately relive the pain of a situation they wish they had handled differently. To relive the day in question would be an opportunity to release the grip of guilt and regret.

On the other end of the spectrum are people who had happy, carefree childhoods punctuated by moments of fun and adventure. People in this category would probably have a hard time picking just one day to relive.

As you reflect on this question, remember that this is just another way to think about your approach to life. Are you a person who second-guesses yourself and walks into the future with one eye firmly focused on the past? Or do you welcome adventure, brush off adversity, and keep both eyes planted on the future? Knowing your natu-

ral tendency is important because opportunities to question yourself, your worth, and your sanity abound in the job market. Do your best to view the process as a game. That way, you can learn from your mistakes without taking the process too personally.

What would you change about your childhood if you could?

Here again, your answer might range from "I wish I had started guitar lessons when I was seven" to "It would have been nice to grow up with parents who were loving rather than abusive." Whateve your answer, it is never too late to remember that you have a responsibility to be your own best friend. If learning to play the guitar is still a goal, save money and treat yourself to a few lessons. Set aside time to practice—even if it means waking up earlier. You are never too busy to do what your heart desires. As my mom always said, "Busy people make time."

On the other hand, if you spent your entire childhood focusing on tennis, ice-skating, gymnastics, violin, or some other activity to the exclusion of all else, you may harbor feelings of a lost childhood and missed opportunity. If so, it probably wouldn't make sense to pursue a career that will require 80 to 100 hours per week for the foreseeable future. Instead, you might consider taking time to play and explore. For ideas on this, read *The Backdoor Guide to Short Term Job Adventures* by Michael Landes.

If what you would change about your childhood has more to do with a lack of love and support at home, it doesn't mean you are unworthy. It means you have to work that much harder to love and honor yourself.

To help you along the journey, read *The Art of Happiness: A Handbook for Living* by His Holiness the Dalai Lama and Howard C. Cutler, M.D. This amazing book provides practical advice and insight for people who want to learn to be more compassionate with themselves.

❓ What would you change about your life?

At any given time there are decisions you can make or change that will alter the course of your life. While there are countless people who dream about making changes, too few take action. My friend Kim is an exception. After graduating from Purdue with a degree in management, Kim moved to Chicago. Rather than pursue a business career, she chose to follow her heart. As a result, her lifelong love for swimming led to a job as aquatics director at a local health club. Kim knows herself well enough to realize that she is motivated by happiness rather than money.

Even though she loves her job, Kim recently made the life-changing decision to move to Colorado, where she knows almost no one. When she packed her car, she had no job and no apartment but didn't seem the least bit hesitant. Quite the contrary. She said, "If I waited until I had everything in order, I'd never leave." When asked what she would do for work, Kim said, "I really don't know. I'd love to get another job as an

> If you board the wrong train, it is no use running along the corridor in the other direction.   —*Dietrich Bonhoeffer*

aquatics director. I'm not worried about it, though. I've loved all my jobs. I always seem to find myself surrounded by fun and interesting people." With a positive attitude like that, it's no mystery that she would find enjoyment almost anywhere.

School

Unlike the family specific questions above, I have been asked every question below related to schools. While some questions might not appear to relate to the job search, they are often asked in interviews to learn more about you as a person or to gauge how you think. Although we'll talk more about the interviewing process later, it's important to do the self-analysis with an eye toward how you might handle the questions in an interview. In this sense, they will provide a sneak preview into corporate recruiting tactics.

❓ What did you enjoy most about each school/experience?

An interviewer who asks this question often does so to learn more about you as a person and to see just how positive and optimistic you are. So, no matter how much

> What we have to learn to do, we learn by doing.　　　—*Aristotle*
>
> I am always ready to learn although I do not always like being taught.
> 　　　—*Sir Winston Churchill*
>
> . . . that is what learning is. You suddenly understand something you've understood all your life, but in a new way.　　　—*Doris Lessing*
>
> A professor is one who talks in someone else's sleep.　　　—*W. H. Auden*

you disliked grade school, high school, or college, find something positive, meaningful, and truthful to say about the experience.

For example, I was fortunate to attend Ogden School, a public grade school in downtown Chicago that was naturally integrated. The boundaries of the school district included low-income housing projects, elite condominiums on Lake Shore Drive, and everything in between. To make matters even more interesting, a wide range of overseas consulates gave the school an international flavor. In a very real sense, we were all different. But while others might have focused on our differences, we focused on our similarities. We were children laughing, learning, and playing together. To this day,

some of my closest friends are people I met at Ogden.

As life goes on, I often think back to my experiences at Ogden. Over the years, I've met more than a few people who, out of sheer ignorance, hold racist, elitist, and anti-Semitic beliefs. It's truly sad. It also makes me grateful for my own childhood experiences. If nothing else, this question can make you appreciate the situations and events that shape the person you are today.

❓ How did you choose the college/graduate school you attended?

This question often comes up in interviews. One company I know uses this question to assess strategic thinking and problem-solving ability. Interviewers who probe in this area often want to hear about your criteria (e.g., availability of certain majors, location, cost) in comparing and contrasting different schools. Since most competitive high schools have counselors who coach college bound students, it isn't hard to remember the process. Strategic thinking comes into play when students finally decide where to apply. Usually the list includes "reach" schools where admission is not guaranteed and "safety" schools where admission is almost certain.

For students who spend the time and money researching and visiting schools, answering this question in an interview won't be difficult. However, since this is not always the case, the question doesn't always work to a candidate's advantage. Some people, for a variety of reasons, don't do an exhaustive search and selection process. For example, many high school seniors are encouraged or expected to attend the alma mater of one of their parents. In this case, they may apply for "Early Decision" and know their fate before even having to apply to other schools.

Other students, for family or financial reasons, attend state schools or universities relatively close to home. Whatever the case, the fact that they didn't have a wide range of colleges to choose from doesn't necessarily make their reasoning less strategic. But it does mean they will have to find another way to demonstrate this important quality. If you find yourself in this category, once you have answered the question and explained the constraints you may have faced, it wouldn't be inappropriate to follow up by saying, "If you asked that question to assess my strategic thinking, I have a number of other examples that provide more insight into how I think, evaluate choices, and approach problems."

If you do this, just make sure you've got the examples to back yourself up. Once you complete the upcoming section on problem solving, you should have ample ideas.

❓ If you could change anything about any school you attended, what would it be and how might you go about doing it?

This is an important question because it demonstrates that you not only recognize problems with management and structure, but also are able to come up with realistic and interesting ideas for improvement. When considering this question, think about the social life as well as the academic life. After all, social life on campus is every bit as important in terms of the overall experience. For many people, what makes college a valuable experience is the maturation process that takes place when they live away from home—often for the first time—and begin to blossom socially and intellectually. Taking this one step further, what good is a straight A average if you can't hold a conversation?

❓ Overall, was school enjoyable and challenging or easy and boring?

The answer to this question may provide an interesting foreshadowing to your professional life. If you are one of those people who were easily bored by school, it is in your best interest to be especially diligent as you research potential careers.

When you first begin your career exploration, ask everyone you meet what keeps them challenged. Once you've narrowed down your career path, ask this question of people who are already in comparable jobs. You may find that projects that started as fresh and inspiring can become rote fairly quickly. You may also find that some companies are better than others about keeping employees challenged and happy. Whatever the case, just make sure you have realistic expectations. Later, if you find you're no longer challenged, use it as your signal to move on.

Social interaction

❓ Why do people like you?

This might seem like a basic, straightforward question, but a lot of people haven't given it much thought. For many, the answer often depends on the depth and quality of their friendships. You may look for different qualities in a drinking buddy than in a confidant. Or you may not. Now, take this one step further and see if you can determine what different friends see in you. Are you a good listener? A source of laughter and adventure? A person with a wide range of interests and abilities? How does this impact the way you interact with people? Are you the same with everyone? Is there a side of you that only certain friends have seen?

If you've traveled extensively and spent long periods living in foreign countries, you have probably gained a deep appreciation of what it takes to interact effectively with people in different cultures. Don't take this for granted, because the ability to embrace cultural diversity is a strong selling point in almost any career.

You may want to ask some of your friends this question and compare their responses to your own. Once you have a better understanding of why people like you, make sure you find a way to demonstrate those qualities in every interview.

❓ How well do you get along with others? Do people like you instantly or does it take time to get to know you?

Knowing how you come across to people who don't know you is important no matter what career path you choose. Although you don't have to be gregarious and instantly likable to be a successful salesperson, for instance, it certainly doesn't hurt. However, it is important to remember that relationships are not solidified at first impressions. Trust and respect can be earned over time by demonstrating a genuine concern for people.

If you're naturally shy and withdrawn, you may find it beneficial to make an extra effort to build relationships with the people you meet. All too often, I have seen quiet, thoughtful people who have been mistakenly judged as aloof, arrogant, and self-centered. Sometimes the easiest and yet most challenging way to accomplish this is to greet people with a smile. It's amazing how disarming a smile can be.

If you have the ability to get along with a wide range of personalities, this would probably be an asset to leverage in your job search. For example, if you find working with economically disadvantaged people particularly rewarding, there are certain careers, like social work and law, where you could have a positive impact. On the other hand, if you know yourself well enough to know that there are certain types of people you have difficulty relating to, you may want to avoid career choices that would bring this issue to the forefront.

When you're interviewing for a job, don't be afraid to mention any interpersonal strengths that are relevant to the potential employer. For example, if the ability to relate to handicapped, elderly, or underprivileged people comes naturally to you—and it is a skill needed by a potential employer—it isn't bragging to talk about how much you enjoy that type of interaction. By citing specific examples you will make the employer feel that much better about hiring you to do what you do best.

What reasons would people have to dislike or lose respect for you?

When you fully understand the basis for the positive and negative reactions people have to you, you will be in a better position to objectively evaluate the validity of your career choices. For example, if you continually aggravate friends with your inability to keep secrets, you probably wouldn't do well as a psychologist, social worker, doctor, lawyer, or in any other profession that demands client confidentiality. Similarly, if you find it difficult to say no or set limits,

you'll probably want to avoid service professions where clients may take advantage of you.

This question sometimes makes people uncomfortable if they have the unrealistic expectation that everyone should like them. The fact is, there is a lot to be said for the immeasurable but real chemistry that exists between people. Some people are instantly attracted to one another and become best friends. Other are repelled from the moment their eyes meet, even without a rational explanation for their feelings. In between these extremes is the range of positive and negative feelings resulting from ongoing interactions.

Think about the people who know you as an acquaintance, a trusted friend, and anywhere in between. What reasons might they have to dislike you? If they could change anything about you, what would it be? Are you the kind of person who can be counted on for fun and adventure but not moral support? Do you always keep your commitments, or do you at times break appointments or show up late with little or no explanation?

Do you prefer to work by yourself or as part of a team?

Working as part of a team can be incredibly rewarding, but it isn't without its share of headaches. On one hand, teams can be a wonderful source of ideas, resources, and inspiration. They can also easily become contaminated by individual negativity, personality conflicts, and other unwelcome outside influences.

> A leader's job is to make it easy to do the right thing and difficult to do the wrong thing. —*Unknown.*

The best team players and leaders recognize obstacles and do their best to keep everyone focused on the same goals. In almost any environment, accomplishments seem to multiply when people work together and encourage each other. In the past, this spirit of teamwork could be seen most often when people worked in the same office. Now, thanks to the Internet and videoconferencing, people from all over the world routinely work together on projects.

Whether you choose to work independently or as part of a team is completely up to you. But whatever you do, be true to your preferences. Once you know what you want, make sure you pursue opportunities that are consistent with your objectives.

Do you do any volunteer work or community service? If so, what do you like best about it?

If you talk to people who have been doing volunteer work for any length of time, you will be struck by the way they talk about it. Contrary to what some people believe, volunteering is not a sacrifice. Far from it. More often than not, volunteers find their efforts so rewarding that they get more out of it than they put in. That's exactly the way it should be. When you're doing something you are truly passionate about, it doesn't feel like work.

From a job hunting perspective, there are quite a few additional benefits to volunteering. For example, volunteering provides a wonderful opportunity to network because it puts you in touch with people from a wide range of backgrounds and professions. The more time you spend supporting an organization you believe in, the more likely it is that people will get to know what a kind, caring, compassionate person you are. From a networking standpoint, what more could you want?

Finally, it's important to remember that volunteer work is exactly the kind of activity that impresses potential employers—especially when it demonstrates a long-term commitment. When you think about it from the employer's point of view, this makes sense. Anyone who has spent considerable time helping the less fortunate is probably a person who possesses an abundance of integrity, wisdom, and patience. Who wouldn't want someone with those qualities on their team?

Are you more comfortable as a leader or as a follower?

Although no one starts out in a leadership position, it's important to factor this question into your long-term planning. If your goal is to run your own company or division, you will do well to commit yourself to a path of ongoing education in the field of management and personnel relations. If you have no such aspirations, that's fine too. Just make sure you do whatever it takes to become an increasingly valuable asset to your employer.

Having thought about this question, you won't have any trouble when it comes time to interview because you'll already know if you want to position yourself more as a leader or as a team player. The truth is, you can position yourself any way you want as long as it's meaningful to a potential employer. Keep this in mind as you work your way through this book because we'll examine this issue in greater detail in subsequent chapters.

What qualities do you value in a friend? Spouse? Coworker?

Having given thought to the qualities you value, you will be better able to communicate your needs on and off the job. As you move ahead in your job search, it's important to think back to all the personalities you've encountered. Who inspires you most? How do they do it? Do they acknowledge or motivate you in a particular way?

Start by comparing your closest friends. What qualities do these friends have in common? Next, think about your favorite teachers. What did they do to inspire you, challenge you, and keep you motivated? These are the qualities you may want to look for in potential employers. Finally, think about the people you've met who aggravated you the most. Did they share any common characteristics? If so, stay on the lookout for those types of personalities. If you found them in life, you'll almost definitely find them at work.

> I do not want to die . . . until I have faithfully made the most of my talent and cultivated the seed that was placed in me until the last small twig has grown.
> —*Käthe Kollwitz*

In life and at work, people who complement one another often form the best partnerships. In order for this to work, each person must be completely honest about his or her relative strengths and weaknesses. One person's strength cannot overcome another person's weakness if the weaker party is unwilling to admit his or her shortcomings. Conversely, a natural ability is only helpful to the degree that a person is comfortable using it.

Interests and accomplishments

What are your hobbies and interests?

Your hobbies and interests are important because they can provide wonderful examples of your passion, dedication, and ability. Too many people don't think about selling themselves on their accomplishments in this area because they have the mistaken impression that it doesn't matter what they do in their free time, the only thing that matters is what they do on the job. There seems to be an unwritten rule for many people that to

> Television is like an open sewer
> flowing through your living room.
>
> —*Unknown*

put an experience on your résumé or mention it in an interview you must have been paid to do it. God forbid that it should have been fun, interesting, or done of your own volition!

Even though the most meaningful, memorable accomplishments often have nothing to do with a paid position, this in no way diminishes the value of the experience in demonstrating your potential and ability. If, for example, you are an avid scuba diver, you may have gone on to earn Rescue Diver and Dive Master certifications. In either case, there is a leadership component, since advanced certifications imply a certain responsibility for the safety of other divers. Think of it as a transferable skill. If you can lead, motivate, and teach people effectively in one area, it makes sense that with proper training, you could do the same in another.

How do you spend your free time?

When you aren't studying or working, what do you do? Do you exercise regularly? Do you take classes just for the fun of it? Are you learning to play a musical instrument? Do you read books?

It amazes me how many people insist they don't have time to do any of the activities listed above. Yet, if you were to ask what happened on *Friends*, *ER*, or any number of other shows, they would have no trouble describing the last twelve episodes extensively. While I have yet to have an interviewer ask if Sunday's episode of *The Simpsons* was new or a rerun, more than a few have asked about the last book I read or class I took. If you'd be embarrassed by this question, challenge yourself to turn off the television for a few weeks. Then get out and experience life.

What would be your ideal vacation?

Once you figure out how you would spend your ideal vacation, start thinking about when you plan to go. In their book *The Aladdin Factor*, Jack Canfield and Mark Victor Hansen talk about the importance of creating a list of 101 goals. The simple exercise of putting your thoughts in writing has a way of making your mind work unconsciously toward turning those goals into a reality. Be specific. It isn't enough to say that you'd like to go on an African safari. Instead, write down when you plan to go and with whom. Believe it or not, the simple act of quantifying and visualizing your goals can lead to absolute miracles. This works for any goal in any area of your life.

To make this visualization work for your job search, write down exactly where you want to work, what your title will be, and a date by which you will be working. You might even take this one step further by creating the likeness of the company's business card on your computer. Once you've put your name and title on the card, print it out and tape it to your bathroom mirror. Or use the image as a screen saver. When you do this, it's important to imagine that you've already achieved your objective. Then, every time you see the image, say a prayer of thanks for having achieved the goal. As Napoleon Hill said, "Whatever the mind can conceive and believe, it can achieve."

What accomplishment gives you the most pride?

It is amazing how often people neglect to sell themselves on this point. More often than not, what gives people the most pride has nothing to do with work or anything they have been paid to do. Instead, the accomplishment relates to an activity they are passionate about. For example, I once coached a client who was proud of her fund-raising work on behalf of Children's Memorial Medical Center in Chicago. Since her answer was a bit vague, I challenged her to consider how her involvement had a measurable impact on her group's fund-raising success. To my surprise, she told me about an idea she had that doubled the attendance and doubled the amount of money raised at an annual fund-raiser. When I probed further, she revealed how she first had to convince the organization's board of directors to implement the idea.

To this day I remember this person for the strength of this one idea and her ability to sell it through the ranks. There are people who work their whole life and never make that kind of impact. Nevertheless, she remained reluctant to put it on her résumé.

To her, it felt like bragging. I disagree. To describe honestly an idea that raised an additional $20,000 for a good cause is simply a statement of fact, not bragging. It is also a strong selling point because it gets potential employers to think, "If she can do that for them, just think what she will be able to accomplish for us."

Job History/Preferences

Have you ever had a job?

If you have never had a job, don't worry. Entry-level positions, by definition, don't require experience. Whether you have had a job or not, you will still have to demonstrate potential. You can do this by citing other accomplishments, including summer jobs, internships—even your leadership or involvement on a team, club, or fund-raising activity.

A few years ago I met a recent graduate who wanted to become a writer. Like many recent graduates and job hunters, the most memorable and compelling fact demonstrating his potential was not prominent on his résumé. Fortunately, he did have a listing for the "Twin Cities to Chicago AIDS Ride," an annual fund-raiser in which thousands of bike riders travel from Minneapolis–St. Paul to Chicago.

To assess his true level of interest and commitment, I asked him how much money he raised. I was shocked when he said, "Over $10,000." I probed deeper, and discovered that, rather than ask family and friends to sponsor his ride, Mark put together a list of about 100 acquaintances who were successful businesspeople. These were not people he knew particularly well, just people he'd met at some point. Then he wrote a colorful letter explaining the objective of the ride and asking for their financial support. Almost twenty-five people responded with donations. Not satisfied, Mark waited a few months and sent a follow-up letter to the people who didn't respond. In the final analysis, 47 percent responded.

What Mark didn't realize is that direct mail fund-raising is a big business in which a 2 or 3 percent response rate is considered successful. A 47 percent response is nothing short of phenomenal. I encouraged him to revise his résumé to highlight this achievement. This became a crucial selling point because it provided solid, believable evidence that Mark was a gifted, creative writer who could persuade people with his words.

Why did you take the job?

Except for those fortunate enough to be independently wealthy, the main reason most people take any job is to earn money, and there are as many ways to make money as there are reasons for needing it. So, you'll have to dig deeper into your psyche and examine various facets of your work life. Were you looking for extra spending money, rent money, or money for your education?

You'll need to be clear about your reason for taking each job for two reasons. First, you may be able to use the job as a way to demonstrate your ability to set and

> The best career advice to give to the young is "Find out what you like doing best and get someone to pay you for doing it." —*Katherine Whitehorn*

achieve goals. For example, if you were looking for extra spending money to finance a trip overseas, you can use the job as a way to demonstrate your resolve. That may not seem like a huge selling point to you, but it is. Many people simply don't have the discipline or motivation to conceive and stick to goals.

The other reason to be clear about your reason for taking each job is more strategic. For example, if you had a series of jobs that are completely unrelated to your career goal, you might appear unfocused—even if your goal was to make money rather than gain experience. Fortunately this is an easy perception to correct. When you list these jobs on your résumé, create a separate section and give it a title that explains why you did what you did. Such as, "How I Put Myself Through College" or "How I Financed My Goal of Backpacking Around the World."

How did you get the job?

How you went about getting a job may not seem important at first blush, but it is, because it can demonstrate resourcefulness, perseverance, your ability to network, and any number of other valuable traits.

If you responded to an ad or approached an employer without any contacts, you must have done something to impress the company or you wouldn't have been hired. If so, what did the company need and how did you convince the hirer you were the right person for the job? If you heard about the position through a friend or networking contact, you can safely add this to your list of examples that demonstrate resourcefulness. If you were recruited for the position, how did the company find you? Even if you don't know the exact answer to this question, the simple fact that you were recruited suggests that you have a reputation as a capable, valuable employee.

What were your job responsibilities?

Take time to reflect on your initial responsibilities. Did you meet or exceed expectations? Were you given more responsibility over time? Were you recognized for any achievements? Did you earn a raise? Raises, honors, and additional responsibilities are indisputable, factual ways to demonstrate that an employer valued your contributions. Make sure you find a way to leverage this. It's amazing how many people don't.

I'll never forget the candidate who had an internship with a travel magazine. As often happens, he didn't take the time to highlight his most impressive accomplishments on his résumé. Instead, like most people, he just listed the internship with the dates next to the name of the magazine. When I asked him what he liked best about the internship, I was shocked to hear that

they had sent him on special assignments to Kenya, Hawaii, Kentucky, and Minnesota. Later, when the assistant editor resigned, the magazine asked him to be the temporary assistant editor until a permanent replacement could be found. You can't get a much better endorsement than that. Only when I reminded him that most interns rarely get special assignments more involved than picking up a pizza was I able to convince him to list the experience on his résumé.

What did you learn in each job?

How are you a more valuable asset to current and future employers? Are there particular skills you developed along the way? Did the company send you for any advanced training sessions? Did your ability to handle difficult or disagreeable people improve? What did you enjoy most about the position? Were you surrounded by talented, wonderful people? Were you constantly challenged? Did you learn more than you ever expected?

In any job, make it a habit to keep a private file of accomplishments. Every time you make an impact, exceed expectations, or receive a compliment, record it in this file. Also, keep track of your ideas—especially the ones you are able to implement. This information will be invaluable at your performance review. Your record keeping will also simplify your life when it comes time to update your résumé.

Conversely, what did you dislike about the position? Even the most miserable experiences have lessons to teach us. Always take time to think about what you would

> The heart has its reasons which reason does not know. —*Blaise Pascal*

change and how you might change it. How could you have been more effective? Are there any questions you'd now ask in an interview that you wouldn't necessarily have asked before? What do you know now that you wish you knew when you started? Keeping these questions in mind can help you avoid repeating the same mistakes in the future.

Would you consider relocating?

While you might be willing to move across the country for a great position, not everyone is. For this reason, it's important to communicate these preferences in your cover letter or on your résumé. While no one will hire you for this reason alone, it can be a strong selling point when the match is already good.

Would you like to work overseas? If so, what relevant skills can you offer your employer?

Again, look beyond the obvious. If you want to work in Italy and you already speak Italian, that's great. But what else can you offer? Do you have any experience interacting with Italians on a business level? Have you ever worked and lived in Italy? Have you ever worked anywhere overseas? Even

if you haven't lived in Italy, you may be able to use a related experience to convince an employer that you have the potential to excel in the position.

Motivations/Goals

How do you stay motivated?

Not everyone can stay motivated for long periods of time. How do you stay focused on your goals during those difficult periods when monotony or boredom inevitably appears?

Even the most focused people occasionally struggle with periods when they lack inspiration and motivation. Are you someone who loves to get up and exercise every day? Do you enjoy exercise most of the time and force yourself to do it the rest of the time? Or do you just skip the workout when you're not feeling motivated? For many people the best cure for resistance is to start doing whatever it is that they've been putting off.

In the job hunting process, resistance and procrastination are especially common because fear and uncertainty are a natural part of the process. When you haven't done it before, it's going to feel uncomfortable at first. If you find yourself struggling with this issue, take time to explore and understand your feelings. Give yourself permission to learn and make mistakes. Olympic runners weren't born wearing track shoes. Like everyone else, they fell repeatedly before they ever took their first steps. The same is true in the job search. Focus on progress rather than perfection. Progress will happen. Perfection won't.

If you could spend your life doing anything (career-oriented) and money wasn't an issue, what would you do?

Ask yourself this question from time to time and see if the answer changes. Whatever you do, don't censor your answers. Too many people cut themselves off because their rational mind tells them they can't make a living doing what they love. Don't make that mistake.

If you could only accomplish one goal in life, what would it be?

This is yet another question designed to help you access your innermost desires. Once you've answered this question, the next logical question is, "What are you waiting for?" Don't assume you have the rest of your life to procrastinate. If you're committed to a particular goal, the time to take action is now. After all, what could be more important than your number one goal?

The benefit of taking action toward a goal is that the universe has a way of conspiring to help you meet your goals once you have taken action. But it won't happen if you don't take the first step. Almost anyone who has committed to a goal without knowing exactly how it will take shape can tell you story after story about the "coincidences" that happened along the way. The longer I live, the less I believe in coincidence. Everything happens for a reason. But it doesn't happen to people who sit around and wait. It happens to people who press forward focused on their goal.

Why do you want to work in a particular industry?

Once you have decided on a particular career path, make sure you have good, solid reasons for doing so. Too many people have romantic ideas about particular careers from watching movies and television shows that have little or no basis in reality. Before you commit to a career or course of study, take time to meet and interview as many people in that career as possible. Shadow people for a day. Offer to work for a few weeks without pay just to gain exposure to the industry. This will help you make an informed decision.

What other careers have you considered, even briefly?

If you're like many people, you have considered a variety of potential careers. What are those other ideas? Have you taken the time to research each one thoroughly? If you're still in school, this is the best time to find and interview people in a variety of careers. Later we'll talk more about informational interviews. In the meantime, just be aware that you can use the alumni network at your school to find people in different industries. You'll be amazed how willing people are to help.

What are your short-, medium-, and long-term goals?

Make a list of your goals. Most people don't do this, either formally or informally, but it can have a significant, positive impact on your productivity.

Taking the time to sort your goals according to the time frames in which they can be achieved is important because not every goal can be achieved this week, this month, or this year. Once you have a clear picture of your current goals, outline the steps that must be taken in order to achieve them. In this way you will begin to develop a realistic time frame for each goal. For example, if you're a college senior with the goal to be CEO of a Fortune 100 technology company, you'd have to acquire more than a little professional experience before you had the track record of success to qualify for the job. Realistically, you'd have to list this as a long-term goal with relevant short- and medium-range goals that lead up to it.

In the example above, a series of short-term goals specifically related to your goal of becoming CEO would be appropriate. For example, a great first step would be to make a list of executives you admire and learn about the steps each took to achieve comparable goals. A related medium-range goal might involve gaining management experience at a range of different companies, including manufacturers, suppliers, and resellers of high-tech equipment and services. In an area that changes as quickly as technology, you'll have to continually monitor the industry and plan your moves accordingly.

> He who would learn to fly one day must first learn to stand and walk and run and climb and dance; one cannot fly into flying.
> —*Friedrich Nietzsche*
>
> Nothing is more permanent than you make it. —*Marie Dilger Hartmann*

As you go through this exercise, it's important to ask yourself how you'd feel having achieved each goal, and what your life would look like when you did. For example, if you are attracted by the power and wealth associated with running a large multinational corporation and your true passion is painting, it may be unrealistic to think you will have adequate time to devote to both. Nevertheless, by going through this exercise you'll be able to create a picture of what you want to accomplish in every area of your life and how it all fits together. For this reason, it's important to review and update your goals on a regular basis. Once you know exactly what needs to be done, you'll be in a better position to make it happen.

How does your mind work? Are you particularly analytical? Resourceful? Strategic? Creative?

Understanding the type of person you are is essential as you begin to identify potential career paths. As you take the time to evaluate your strengths and preferences, you will naturally begin the process of matching your talents to the requirements of a particular position. If you consider yourself analytical, challenge yourself to come up with ten examples of analytical thinking. Keep in mind that analytical thinking is not about number crunching as much as it is about the way you analyze and approach challenges.

Imagine, for example, that you have to arrange an office to maximize the number of people it can accommodate without making it so cluttered and cramped that it negatively impacts the effectiveness and morale of the people who have to work there. The process of analyzing, testing, and revising alternatives and coming up with new solutions would be considered analytical thinking. As part of the process, you might research space management software programs or consult a feng shui expert. Any part of the process that expands your alternatives and helps you make a more educated decision can be factored in as an example of analytical thinking. The alternatives you uncover may also be considered examples of

strategic thinking, problem solving, and resourcefulness.

Once you have finished listing examples of one trait, repeat the exercise for every quality that describes you. For each example, remember how you felt at the time. Were you challenged and happy, bored and unhappy, or somewhere in between? This is important because many people have valuable skills and talents they don't enjoy using on a daily basis.

What are your professional objectives?

As you look to the future, ask yourself what you're working toward. Are you content with making a living while building and maintaining excellent personal relationships, or are you committed to leaving your imprint on the world? In a world that focuses on success and upward mobility, we sometimes lose sight of the fact that a significant percentage of the population is content in what they're doing. This contentment can be a huge selling point. In fast-paced industries where people compete for promotions, keeping jobs filled—especially at the lower levels—can be difficult. That's why companies are often thrilled to find employees who aren't looking for additional responsibility.

You may be wondering if you fit this description. If so, ask yourself the following questions: Do you prefer the predictability of dealing with the same people, projects, and challenges? Does the possibility of having your supervisor's job hold little or no attraction? Do you prefer to work inde-

> Life is what happens to you while you're busy making other plans.
>
> —*John Lennon*

pendently without anyone reporting to you? If you answered yes to these questions, you may be just this type of person. If so, it can be a selling point you wouldn't want to miss.

Work Ethic

Are you organized? Detail-oriented? Punctual?

As you embark on the job search, it's important to know what your tendencies are. Of these three, punctuality is one of the most common pitfalls for job hunters. Delays inevitably arise, so allow for extra time. It's always less stressful to do your waiting in the company's office than it is to be stuck in traffic, frantically looking for a parking space, or waiting for the train. If it's apparent that you'll be more than ten minutes late, call ahead. In this age of cell phones, it's simply inexcusable to keep people waiting without word from you. Although the issues of organization and attention-to-detail are more relevant on the job, it is important to take steps to correct any issues you might have in these areas.

What would previous employers identify as your greatest strengths?

To market yourself effectively, it's important to put modesty aside and ask yourself what makes you a valuable employee. Do you always exceed expectations? Do you consistently find ways to make life easier and more pleasant for the people on your team? Are you a respected leader? Are you the person people count on for ideas? Are you someone who can turn a problem into an opportunity? Have you found ways to save the company money without sacrificing quality or service? What is it that makes you an asset to the team?

It isn't enough to say that you are an idea generator. Have specific examples. If you saved the company money, know exactly how much you saved. If you helped the company make more money, how much did you add to the bottom line? Quantify your personal and professional achievements wherever possible.

What areas do you think you need to improve upon?

This is an important question and one that is often asked in interviews. Are you too short tempered? Do you get frustrated easily? Do you sometimes let personality issues get in the way of your team's objectives? Do you need to work on punctuality? Could your writing and presentation skills benefit from focused attention? If you've already had a job, look at past evaluations for specific ideas to help you answer this question.

Another way to approach this question is to think back to situations you would

> The only place where success comes before work is a dictionary.
>
> —*Unknown*

> Work expands so as to fill the time available for its competition.
>
> —*Cyril Northcote Parkinson*

> They say hard work never hurt anybody, but I figure why take the chance. —*Former President Ronald Reagan (attributed)*

> No one on their deathbed ever said, "Gosh, if only I'd spent more time at the office."
>
> —*Unknown*

handle differently given the opportunity. What does this tell you about yourself? Are there any consistencies across situations? For example, if you were more detail-oriented and organized, would that eliminate any of the issues you have identified?

To help you with this exercise, ask the other people on your team or with whom you work closely. Tell them you're committed to improving and would welcome the opportunity to hear their thoughts about what you do well and what you could do better. As long as you approach the topic constructively and openly, people will generally share their observations. Just remember to be grateful rather than defensive—especially if you don't agree. If you honestly have no idea what your colleagues are talking about,

ask for specific examples. Be careful how you do this. You will get much more constructive feedback if you say, "If you could, help me understand what you mean by sharing a specific example." That is infinitely more pleasant than, "What's that supposed to mean?" or some equally confrontational approach.

❓ When handling involved projects, would you rather focus on the big picture or manage the details? Why?

People generally fall into one category or the other on this issue. Either they are great with details or they have a better grasp of the big picture. Even people who do both well usually enjoy one more than the other.

Although the projects differ, entry-level people in most careers have to learn the details of the business at a project level before they can advance. Since there are no shortcuts for this process, it makes sense that the best managers know exactly what is involved with every project because they have done it themselves. If you don't know how much time and effort is involved, you'll have a more difficult time managing the process.

Personality

❓ What do you like most about yourself?

Are you most proud of your ability to get along with people from a wide range of cultural and socioeconomic backgrounds? Are

> Instead of being *in* the moment, you stood *outside* the moment and judged it. Then you re-acted. That is, you acted as you *did once before*.
> Now look at these two words:
> REACTIVE
> CREATIVE
> Notice they are they same word. Only the "C" has been moved! When you "C" things correctly, you become Creative, rather than Reactive.
> —*from the book* Conversations with God *by* Neale Donald Walsch

> When you and your wife have an argument, regardless of who's wrong, apologize. Say, "I'm sorry I upset you. Would you forgive me?" These are healing, magical words.
> —*from* Life's Little Instruction Book *by* H. Jackson Brown, Jr.

you especially good with children? Animals? The elderly? Are you a great athlete? A talented musician? An expert in a particular area? Have you overcome a difficult obstacle? Can you laugh at yourself or make others laugh? What makes you smile?

What is the most important lesson you have learned?

More often than not, the most valuable lessons come from personal experience. Such lessons can have a profound impact on how we market ourselves and to whom. On a personal note, one of the most important lessons I learned about myself is just how important it is for me to be doing something where I feel I'm having a positive impact on someone else's quality of life. Not surprisingly, I never got that feeling on the trading floor of the Chicago Board of Trade. Nor did I experience it working in advertising. As with any passion, this commitment to making a difference plays a huge role in marketing myself as a speaker and writer because it helps people realize that I care deeply about what I do.

What are your objectives in your personal life? On the job?

Are you absolutely driven to achieve certain professional goals, or are you more focused on personal goals? Do you plan to start a family at some point? If so, where will this fit on your list of priorities? Having a meaningful family life and a satisfying career are not mutually exclusive. The challenge is to make time for both. I saw an interview with the CEO of Cisco Systems, one of the most successful computer networking companies, in which he listed his family as his first, second, and third priorities. That's so nice to hear. Too often, high-powered execs and others lose sight of what is really important in life.

In many ways, people are working harder than ever, but it's also nice to see that they're also working smarter. While working as a headhunter and talking with thousands

> The universe is transformation; our life is what our thoughts make it.
>
> —*Marcus Aurelius*
>
> You don't get to choose how you're going to die. Or when. You can only decide how you're going to live. Now.
>
> —*Joan Baez*

of job hunters, I was pleasantly surprised to see a renewed focus on the quality of life. Most people are no longer willing to do anything and everything to gain advancement in salary and title. Instead, more people are actively pursuing opportunities that provide the flexibility to work at home, part-time, or on a freelance basis.

What is your most prized possession?

Is your most prized possession something that would be valuable to anyone, or is it more symbolic? How did you come to have it in your possession? Was it a gift, or something you earned through hard work? Under what circumstances would you be willing to part with this possession? If you were going to give it to someone, who would that be? Why? Is it even something that can be transferred?

For people who grew up in families with parents who did not go to college, a university degree may be their most prized pos-session because of the hard work and sacrifice it represents. For others, their most prized possession may be an heirloom that once belonged to a favorite parent, grandparent, aunt, or uncle. Whatever the case, your most prized possession probably says a lot about what you value in life. The question is, what does it say?

Problem Solving

What are the biggest challenges you have overcome in your personal life and on the job? What steps did you take? What did you learn?

Everyone, at some level, has challenges he or she struggles to overcome. For some, the challenges are physical or biological, while for others the challenges are more situational. Whatever the challenge, by working hard to overcome it, you have emerged a stronger person. The case study "Rethinking Our Dilemmas" shows how a person did just this.

Given the chance to start over, how might you handle these challenges differently? How did the outcome impact others? Did you create a win-win situation for all parties? Was anyone left feeling powerless or disappointed? Are you satisfied with the results? How might you improve your performance?

These questions apply primarily to situations and conflicts that arise between people. At some point, everyone has been involved in a misunderstanding or disagreement. But not everyone has learned from the experience. Some people just seem to get more stubborn and disagreeable with each passing moment. Others take time to assess their role with as much objectivity as possible. In this way, they are able to use every experience as another opportunity to teach themselves to think rather than react.

One of the most valuable lessons any of us can learn is to agree to disagree. By perfecting this skill, we can disagree without being disagreeable. This can be especially useful in the workplace, where people often have conflicting ways to approach particular projects and challenges. When this happens, it's important for everyone to step back and remind each other that they are working toward the same goal. It's also helpful to remember not to take the disagreements personally. Just saying, "It's always business, never personal," can do a lot to ease tension.

What challenges have you faced that have not been resolved to your satisfaction? What opportunities do you have to improve the situation? Are you taking action to resolve the issues? Why or why not?

At times life is all about overcoming obstacles. At any given moment, it seems, there are challenges to face. Some issues are more pressing than others and require immediate attention. Others, for better or worse, can be ignored indefinitely.

Some people, in their continual effort to avoid confrontation, allow these skeletons to accumulate in their closets. Given the negative impact this has on health and happiness, ignoring the issues is not a good idea. Whatever the challenge, there is something incredibly liberating about dealing with it. Scary at times, but also liberating.

If there are issues you haven't faced, consider making a list of pros and cons outlining the price you pay by ignoring the problem versus what you would gain by taking steps to resolve it. This exercise can provide the impetus to do what needs to be done. If not, figure out what would. Remember, you don't have to wait until you have absolutely certainty that your efforts will solve the problem. If you did, you would never get started. Instead, your reward will be the inner strength you discover by taking action.

Rethinking Our Dilemmas

A few years back, a woman I'll call Kara came to me because she was having trouble getting past an initial interview with any firm. As Kara described how she had moved to progressively larger architectural firms with greater responsibility, I couldn't escape the feeling that she was hiding something. Since she was exceptionally bright and had solid examples of her experience, I didn't have any reason to question her ability. Nevertheless, her entire demeanor gave me the uncomfortable feeling she wasn't being completely forthright about her background. To complicate matters even further, Kara had a year-long gap on her résumé that she clearly didn't want to discuss. Together, these facts were more than enough for an employer to decide she wasn't worth the risk.

Ordinarily, résumé gaps don't concern me because they usually have little or no impact on the person's ability to do the job. As such, it really doesn't make any difference if the person was sailing the Indian Ocean, hospitalized with a broken leg, or holding out for the perfect job. However, in this case, because of the way Kara avoided the issue, I knew it held the key to solving her job-hunting issues. For the first forty-five minutes of our meeting, I worked hard to build her trust. First, I probed for factual examples of quantitative ability, problem solving, and other qualities important in her chosen field. Once I had established a level of rapport, Kara knew that I genuinely wanted to help. Making it clear I wasn't there to make a judgment, I proceeded to share my candid impressions. I didn't ask for an explanation, I just asked her to think about what I said.

Kara took a deep breath, shifted nervously in her chair, and began to share her story. For years, Kara had struggled with the eating disorder anorexia nervosa. At first, she did her best to deal with it on her own. When that didn't work, she joined support groups. Despite her efforts, the disorder continued to disrupt her life. Eventually, Kara realized that she wasn't doing her employer or herself any favors. Without looking back, Kara checked herself into a full-time rehabilitation program and spent the next year regaining her health.

As I listened in amazement, I was simultaneously inspired by Kara's courage and struck by her fear that other people might find out what hap-

continued

The Self-Assessment 55

pened and hold it against her. I viewed the situation differently. Kara's decision to quit work and deal with her health problems actually demonstrated enormous integrity.

Faced with the same dilemma, the average person would probably be so afraid of losing a steady paycheck and health insurance that he or she would keep working until his or her performance suffered enough to result in dismissal. Kara didn't do that. When she recognized that her disorder was having a negative impact on her work, Kara confronted the issue directly. Every employer should be so fortunate. Every person should be so proactive.

By rethinking and looking at her experience from a broader perspective, Kara learned to view her recovery as an asset rather than a liability. On their own, obstacles and challenges don't automatically have any significance. It's not what happened, but what we learn about ourselves that ultimately gives it meaning. And that is always up to us.

Redefining the Résumé

According to the *Oxford English Dictionary*, the word *résumé* is loosely defined as a brief account of one's educational and professional experience. Unfortunately, this is the limit of most thinking on the topic. As a result, we have a society with a penchant for writing résumés so generic they could describe anyone yet sell no one. So, how should we think about résumés? I propose an alternate, job-hunter-specific definition:

Your life, summarized on one or two pages, as it relates specifically to what you want to do.

Every job hunter, whether a seasoned professional or a recent graduate, should approach the job search as a game of strategy. The object of the game is to match potential (not necessarily experience) with the requirements of a particular employer. Because these requirements tend to be specific, the typical résumé is often useless. For example, if a company is looking for people with analytical ability, problem-solving

> No task is a long one but the task on which one dare not start. It becomes a nightmare. —*Charles Baudelaire*

skills, and the ability to deal with difficult people, a laundry list of previous employers and job titles is not going to convince the hiring manager to bring you in for an interview. Fortunately, there are better ways to demonstrate your potential.

Why the focus on potential? Many job hunters, career changers, and entry-level candidates don't have previous work experience. However, that doesn't mean they lack potential. Too many people miss this important distinction, and as a result they waste valuable time apologizing for their lack of experience. To the potential employer, this is not a selling point.

How many times have you heard someone say, "We're looking for someone with x year(s) of experience?" Unfortunately, no one ever stops to ask, "What are your expectations of the specific skills and qualifications of someone with the year(s) of experience you require?"

Experience is not a function of time, job title, or profession. It's what you learned that matters, not where you learned it. Recognizing this, it's a lot easier to identify other life experiences—not necessarily work related—that demonstrate comparable relevant skills.

Once you know exactly what an employer is looking for—and how you have

demonstrated potential—you may be surprised just how easy it is to put together a convincing cover letter and résumé. Conversely, unless you know exactly why a potential employer should be interested in you, don't bother to write a résumé.

The Soul-Searching Behind the Résumé

For now, forget about writing a résumé and reflect on the topics and questions below. Most of them deal with what you have done or hope to accomplish. This information is essential if you hope to market yourself effectively. Nevertheless, the answer to the following question is the key to any successful job search:

What skills or qualities are important to a particular employer?

Is it surprising that this has almost nothing to do with you? If, as I suspect, you haven't given this enough attention, don't beat yourself up. Most people don't consider it at all, therefore most people who pursue hard-to-get jobs don't get them either.

Objective

What is your dream job?

Whether or not you know the answer to this question, you owe it to yourself to talk with as many people in as many different careers as possible. If you can, focus on people who love their jobs. They can teach you the most about what to look for in a career because, in all likelihood, they didn't start out in the job they love. They worked toward it. Find out what they learned along the way.

Once you have a career in mind, do your best to learn not only what people enjoy about it, but also what frustrates them. Whatever you do, it's important not to romanticize your career of choice. This way, you can minimize the impact of unpleasant surprises down the road.

What attracts you to this career?

Of all the questions people neglect to ask, this one may be the most common. It isn't enough to be passionately enthusiastic about a particular career if you can't convincingly explain why you're attracted to it. Take the time to explore the origin of your interest. If your reasoning is flighty or unbelievable, you won't be hired. It's that simple.

Let's imagine you've decided to pursue a career in research and development in the toy industry. If you enthusiastically tell an interviewer that you saw the movie *Big* with Tom Hanks and have been dreaming about this career ever since, it won't be convincing. I'm sure the toy industry has been inundated with résumés from people who know nothing about the toy industry beyond what they saw in the movie. And I bet they didn't hire a single one of them.

On the other hand, if you demonstrate your passion by reading the magazines and periodicals that focus on the trade or industry (commonly referred to as the trade press), arranging informational interviews (more about this later), and routinely observing the behavior of children in toy stores, managers will believe your interest is legitimate. The difference is initiative and a realistic outlook. Those who have this are believable. Those who don't are not.

What skills or qualities are important to a potential employer?

By taking the time to read the trade press and conduct informational interviews, you will begin to appreciate the skills that potential employers seek. But remember, every company is different. They have different customers, different products or services, and different corporate cultures. As a result, they also have different needs. Qualities that are important to one employer may be irrelevant or, at worst, detrimental to another. Take time to understand the differences. For example, one company may seek employees who are personally so conservative and corporate that they border on uptight. Other companies may look for employees who are outgoing and free-spirited, while at the same time professional. The same candidate will not appeal to both.

Why would you excel at this career?

The answer to this question is directly related to the prior two questions. Once you have demonstrated the initiative to build a base of knowledge and understanding about the needs of a potential employer, selling yourself will be much easier. Although this may come as a surprise, just having the passion to educate yourself about a particular career is often enough to demonstrate potential—especially at the entry level. The fact is, relatively few people bother to learn anything on their own. It's not as if you need to sign up for extra courses either. Just read everything you can find. If you're genuinely interested in the career, it won't seem like work.

Education

❓ What degrees have you earned?

If you earned an undergraduate degree, how did you choose your major? If your major is related to your chosen profession, feel free to use what you've learned to support your decision. But don't stop there. What prompted you to choose that major in the first place? In my case, I chose to major in psychology because I was fortunate to take two psychology classes in high school from a clinical psychologist. My interest in personality and behavior quickly led to a desire to learn more about consumer behavior. Later, when I interviewed in advertising, I could trace my interest all the way back to high school. In general, the further you can trace your interest and the more you have done to expand it, the more believable it is.

❓ What classes did you take?

Even though you may never use it, challenge yourself to list all of the courses you have taken beyond high school. Next, write down something you learned that wasn't necessarily part of the class. If you're fortunate and aware, you may realize that the most valuable lessons were never outlined in a syllabus. For example, did you have to deal with a professor who was particularly hard on you? Did you find yourself working on group projects with people who didn't always contribute? Through group projects and presentations, you may have learned about dealing with difficult people and working as a team in less than ideal circumstances. All of these learning experiences are relevant, especially if you are applying for a job that requires teamwork.

❓ What classes did you love? What did you learn that you could apply to your future career?

If you are fortunate to have widely varying interests, you may have enjoyed classes that have nothing to do with how you plan to make a living. It's equally possible that some of these classes can provide clues to other possible career paths. Whatever you do, don't ignore the possibilities just because you can't imagine a way to make money in that field. Instead, take the time to talk with your professors, friends, and acquaintances. Ask for ideas. A simple conversation can change your life.

Finding the Gold in Extracurricular Activities

With relatively limited work experiences, entry-level job hunters can often look to extracurricular activities for solid examples that demonstrate their potential. This is perfectly acceptable. To make this meaningful, it's important to describe how the experience demonstrates potential in a way that applies to similar challenges you might face on the job. This might be a universal challenge—such as dealing with difficult people—that would be valuable to any potential employer. It could also be more specific.

Perhaps you handled finances for the student government and determined budget allocation for all on-campus groups. That would certainly provide a solid example of leadership and financial responsibility. Taking this a step further, examine the decisions you made. Did you have virtually unlimited resources, or did the university give you a set budget to divide fairly? Allocating a limited budget would necessarily yield examples of problem solving as you worked to balance the competing needs of different organizations. At the same time, it would almost definitely give you experience convincing unhappy people that your decisions were fair given the circumstances.

The experiences described above can be as valuable to the people in the student organizations as they are to the person who managed the budgets. When I started working at our college radio station, we were under tremendous pressure from the Student Government Association to change our format or lose our funding. For this reason, from an undergraduate life experience perspective, I probably learned the most valuable lessons during the two years I spent as program director of the station.

When I took office, we had what can only be described as an adversarial relationship with the Student Government Association. Since the SGA didn't believe that the station's progressive format appealed to the majority of students, they threatened to eliminate our funding. In response, we worked hard to improve relations with the students and the SGA.

Through campus surveys, format adjustments, and an ongoing public relations effort, we began to change our image. Thanks to tie-dye parties, specialty programming, and live performances, we created awareness about opportunities at the station and gained a loyal following. The next year, our introductory meeting to recruit student disc jockeys, sportscasters, and oth-

continued

ers was standing room only. The previous year, attendance had been abysmal. Best of all, we kept our SGA funding.

To see how an experience like this might relate to other career-related challenges, think of it in more general terms. What was the problem or issue? How did you address it? Do the strategy and tactics apply to a potential employer? In our case, people who were involved in the repositioning effort gained valuable experience in the following areas:

Problem Solving: *Understanding, addressing, and solving the issues surrounding our adversarial relationship with the student government in particular as well as the student body as a whole.*

Consumer Research: *Creating surveys and interviewing students to understand their perceptions about the station. This method was also used to solicit ideas.*

Strategic Thinking: *Creating and implementing a plan to boost popularity without abandoning the progressive format. In the end, a variety of specialty shows were added, including blues, jazz, and classical. We also added a three-hour Grateful Dead show.*

Event Planning: *Organizing and planning live concerts and parties.*

Promotion and Public Relations: *Generating awareness about the format changes and special events the station sponsored to create goodwill and student support.*

While event planning may not be interesting to a particular employer, the ability to think strategically and solve problems probably will be. Know what the employer values, and you'll know what to leverage.

Experience

? List all the jobs, extracurricular activities, travel, and volunteer experiences you've had.

This may seem time consuming, but you only have to do it once. After that, it's simply a matter of updating your list. Before any interview, review this list so the experiences are fresh in your mind. Since you don't know what questions an interviewer will ask, this strategy will give you a huge inventory of examples from which to draw. For each activity, write down how you got started and how long you were involved.

For the travel category, focus on exotic destinations and extended stays. Have you been anywhere or done anything that most people never have the opportunity to do? Have you bungee-jumped in Iceland, parasailed in the Himalayas, or gone scuba diving in the Galapagos Islands? Did you serve in the Peace Corps in Africa, South America, or India? Did you study abroad in Spain, Australia, South Africa, Italy, France, or anyplace else? What did you learn? What surprised you the most about the culture? What was your biggest challenge?

? For each job and volunteer experience, list your responsibilities.

Did your work exceed expectations? Were you entrusted with additional responsibilities? If so, describe them in detail. From an interviewer's standpoint, it is much more interesting to hear specifics than broad generalizations. What, exactly, did you achieve

> Most human beings have an almost infinite capacity for taking things for granted. —*Aldous Huxley*

beyond what was already expected? Were you given supervisory responsibilities? Were you selected to help train new employees or volunteers?

Be sure to include any extracurricular experiences that may be relevant. For example, if you worked on the college radio station, newspaper, or yearbook, think back on the challenges you faced. As pointed out in the case study "Finding Gold in Extracurricular Activities," the experience may prove to be a great example of problem solving, leadership, strategic thinking, resourcefulness, or another equally valuable quality.

? Have you ever earned a raise or promotion?

To be able to say you earned a raise or raises, even in a part-time position, is like having your boss tell an interviewer what a great job you did. The assumption is that you earned the raise through hard work and dedication. The same is true for promotions.

If you worked on your own teaching tennis, sailing, or a musical instrument, you can quantify your experiences by tracking the number of students. How many students did you have when you started? How many students have you taught in total? How many stayed with you for extended periods?

How much did you charge per lesson? Were you able to raise your rates?

For other entrepreneurial ventures, quantify your success through sales or revenue growth. Your ability to market your products or yourself is every bit as valuable as a raise or promotion is to people who work for others.

List any awards you have won.

Like raises and promotions, being recognized by others is another great independent verification of your ability. Don't be hesitant to leverage this. Remember that awards can take many different forms (e.g., trophies, plaques, incentive vacations). Just being nominated for an award is usually worth mentioning. Having an article, story, poem, or research paper published can also be considered an award—especially if the competition was stiff.

Whatever the case, put the award in perspective. How many people were eligible for the honor? What impact did your efforts have on the organization that nominated you? Consider the difference between the following:

Unichem Employee of the Year: *85th Annual Recipient*

Unichem Employee of the Year: *Awarded for ten years of work in the Brazilian rain forest that led to the discovery of a medicinal plant the company is now synthesizing to treat high blood pressure*

By taking the time to describe the circumstances leading up to an award, you can better communicate the importance of the achievement. Recently, I met with a woman who won an Emmy award as an associate producer in Los Angeles. Along the way, she was nominated for three other Emmys. However, I had to practically drag the information out of her. To her, even talking about the awards seemed too much like bragging—especially since it wasn't an individual effort. To help her put the achievement in perspective, I encouraged her to list the award and nominations by category with a brief description of the competition, the key players, and the decision makers. Including a brief list of the people she worked with not only communicated the team nature of the award, but also positioned her as one of the key players. For these reasons, focusing on the facts is a great way to leverage your achievements without coming across as a braggart.

Have you ever held an office or other position in a school, church, or volunteer activity? Were you elected or appointed?

This information is especially valuable to anyone who needs leadership experience to demonstrate the potential to succeed. If you were elected, how many people did you run against? If you were appointed, on what basis was the decision made? What did you do to convince the voters or board members that you were the right person for the position?

Next, think about what you accomplished in the position. Did you seek another term? What could you do to lead even more effectively? How would your supporters describe your leadership style? What would your critics have to say? If you don't know the answer to the last question, find out. Everyone has opportunities for improvement. As much as we might resist our critics, they often have legitimate observations that hold the key to our future growth. But if you never ask, you may never find out.

Outside interests/life experiences

❓ What do you do for enjoyment?

What activities consistently bring you happiness? Are you an avid reader? If so, what type of books do you enjoy most? Fiction? Biography? Self-help? New Age? Are you a person who can spend hours in a bookstore? If not, what would you rather be doing?

In my case, I get an enormous amount of enjoyment from music. I love listening to music, finding new bands, playing guitar, playing piano, seeing concerts, singing—you name it. In a perfect world, I would have enough talent to write songs and play in a band. I might be a dreamer at times, but I'm not delusional enough to think that's a realistic career possibility. If you have the talent and desire to nurture your artistic side and pursue it as a career,

go for it. Few jobs could ever give you as much pleasure and fulfillment. If it doesn't work out, you can always go the corporate route later. You've got your whole life to explore possibilities.

Whatever your interest—even if you can't support yourself doing it full-time—make time for it at least once a week. Otherwise, the weeks will slip into months and years and you'll rob yourself of one of life's greatest enjoyments.

❓ What do you wish everyone knew about you that they might otherwise never know?

Here's an opportunity to acknowledge yourself in a way most meaningful to you. I make a point to ask this question in every interview because it gives people a chance to unself-consciously share interesting facts I would otherwise never know. Learning what gives people the most pride invariably provides a glimpse at what makes them special.

When you answer this question, don't be shy. If this is a difficult task for you, pretend you're a public relations agent representing a client. In this case, the client happens to be you. If you can answer this question with more than one fact, all the better. But come up with at least one. When you have an answer, ask your best friend what he or she wishes everyone knew about you. That should make for an interesting comparison. It might even make you realize that you mean more to others than you imagined.

References

❓ Other than family, who appreciates and respects your talents and abilities?

Favorite teachers, bosses, coworkers, and other people who know your strengths first-hand can be wonderful resources for soul-searching exercises like the ones in this book. Again, you may be surprised by the range of qualities people admire in you.

❓ Who knows what a competent, hardworking person you are?

Have your efforts in any area exceeded expectations? If so, what were the circumstances? Who witnessed and appreciated your hard work? The people who benefited from your efforts are just the ones who probably won't hesitate to give you an enthusiastic endorsement. Make sure you stay in touch or know how to find them. You can never have too many solid references.

❓ What do people see as your greatest strengths? What do they see as your greatest opportunities for improvement?

Once you've answered these questions on your own, ask them of everyone you listed in the previous two questions. People who know your strengths are often equally insightful when it comes to your opportunities for improvement. Friends may love you and enjoy your company, but it doesn't mean they don't recognize your flaws. They sim-ply choose not to focus on them or share unsolicited observations. Remember, just because you don't often ask about your shortcomings doesn't mean they aren't noticed.

Résumé Basics

To better prepare you for the challenge of building your own résumé, this next section features a fictitious undergraduate named Emery McTell. By going through the process through the eyes of another person, the opportunities and pitfalls of résumé writing should be more apparent. Although you and Emery may not share the same professional objectives, you can learn a lot by applying the process to your own situation.

The biographical sketch provides an overview of the experiences from which Emery has to draw in creating a résumé and cover letter appropriate for advertising. Despite the fact that Emery has no prior full-time work experience, she has qualities that smart employers value—passion and initiative. Some people refer to this as a "fire in the belly." Others describe it as "a burning hunger." Whatever it is, she's got it.

In many respects, Emery's background is aspirational. For the truly hungry—the people who get the hard-to-get jobs—it is also achievable. It's important to notice that Emery's experience is a result of her own initiative. There isn't one experience listed that isn't achievable in your own life. It doesn't matter if your talents are not creatively, analytically, or strategically focused.

Biographical Sketch

Name: Emery Stephanie McTell

Age: 21

Sex: Female

Occupation: Student, State University

Major: Communications   **Minor:** Psychology

Graduation: June 2002

Extracurricular Activities: University marketing club, University daily newspaper, WAVO-FM

Career Objective: Marketing Management

Work Experience

Full-time: None

Part-time: Just For Fun Designs (1996–1998) and Spare Time Promotions (1997–Present)

Just For Fun Designs

During her freshman year in high school, Emery became interested in jewelry design. At first she made earrings, bracelets, and watchbands exclusively for herself and her friends. As more people wore the jewelry, demand increased. Before long she found herself spending more time making jewelry just to keep pace with requests. Within eighteen months this activity generated $200 per week in profit. At peak efficiency, Emery only had to work three or four nights a week for two hours and one day every other weekend to meet demand.

The next year, Emery began selling her products to nearby stores under the name Just For Fun Designs. Since she no longer had direct contact with the customer, Emery enclosed a return postcard for people who wanted to be added to the mailing list. Whenever a new store began carrying Just For Fun products, people on the mailing list received an announcement. As her list of satisfied customers grew, so did her distribution network.

Spare Time Promotions

As it happened, Emery had as much fun marketing her products as she did making them. After reading a story about a six-year-old boy who sold bumper

continued

stickers to promote world peace, she wrote to local newspapers with her own story. Her objective was to create awareness so other stores might carry the products. It worked. When the local paper picked up the story, three additional stores asked to carry her products. Emery also began to receive calls from other artists and craftspeople who wanted advice. Recognizing the opportunity to help these people, Emery created Spare Time Promotions.

From a personal standpoint, Spare Time Promotions was even more fulfilling than jewelry design. On the one hand, it helped artists and craftspeople who lacked the skills to market themselves. On the other, it enabled Emery and the other artists to support "Young Artists at Risk" —an art program for lower-income children.

By the time Emery graduated from high school, she had established relationships with fifteen retail outlets in five communities. She also acted as a marketer/distributor for thirty local artisans. Before she left for college, she recruited and trained four younger students to manage production and distribution.

State University Marketing Club

As a communications major/psychology minor, Emery gained a deeper appreciation for marketing and consumer behavior. During her first semester, she joined the marketing club and was disappointed to see that it lacked focus. Except for an occasional guest lecturer, nothing was ever accomplished.

Seeing the possibilities that existed in a group of fifteen enthusiastic, would-be marketers, Emery championed a restructuring of the club. After recruiting faculty sponsors from the psychology, communications, and economics departments, she led a team into the community in search of entrepreneurs and startup companies. Through this project, she created a win-win situation for the companies and students alike. The companies received free marketing assistance. The club members gained experience writing and presenting marketing plans. Students who participated in more involved projects even received academic credit.

Emery was unanimously elected club president as a sophomore. Within three years of the restructuring, active participation had grown from 15 to 105 students. Graduating members were actively recruited by advertising agencies, start-up companies, and others.

University News/Marketing Column

To ensure ongoing media exposure, Emery convinced the university paper to run a weekly marketing column written by the marketing club. The club used the space to promote ongoing and upcoming projects. On occasion, local entrepreneurs wrote special features—usually about their interaction with the marketing club. Three months after the column began, club awareness on campus approached 90 percent. Over 75 percent of the new members surveyed pointed to the column as their first exposure to the club.

Other Extracurricular Activities

Tennis Team: Member (four years)
WAVO-FM: Newscaster/disc jockey (two years)
Special Olympics: Volunteer coach (six years)

Note: The information above is intended as an overview of the fictitious candidate featured in the sample résumés that follow. *This is not a résumé.*

With a little inspiration, you can market any ability or interest. And you'll almost certainly learn more on your own than you would in an internship with a Fortune 500 company. (Contrary to popular opinion, internships are not prerequisites for gainful employment, since most are glorified secretarial positions.)

While it isn't necessary to compare yourself point for point or award for award to Emery or anyone else, you should be able to identify and leverage your own unique selling points. The most difficult part of the process is the self-analysis. Once you've matched your skills with an employer's needs, the cover letter and résumé will flow naturally.

Employment history

Many job applicants are under the erroneous impression that qualifications must relate to past employment rather than personal accomplishment. These people would sooner apologize for their (lack of) employment history than sell themselves on raw talent. This insecurity has two negative consequences. First, time that should be spent preparing is spent procrastinating. Second, the résumé, when it is finally written, is a meaningless collection of facts that could apply to anyone—and sells no one.

This is hazardous for recent graduates, since their achievements are rarely work-related. Entry-level job seekers, in particular, should keep three facts in mind. First, your history, whether it includes full-time employment or not, is just that—history. The past is only useful to the extent that it can be used to demonstrate potential. Second, by definition, entry-level positions are filled by people who have no prior experience. People who have experience in a given field don't compete at the entry level. Finally, employers recruiting for entry-level positions are more interested in potential than experience.

Starting now, forget everything you have heard or believe about résumés. In this section we will examine the structure, assumptions, and details that make résumés ineffective. Then we will begin with a blank page.

The exercises on the following pages are intended as a guide to focus your efforts. Notice that I used the word "focus" rather than "dictate." The all-purpose, one-size-fits-all format is exactly the shortsighted approach that causes problems in the first place. As you work through the chapter, you may find the sample résumés intimidating. That's good. Like it or not, you will be competing against people who have accomplished more in a summer vacation than others do in a lifetime.

The most common résumé problems

Most résumés lack both individuality and focus. Like anyone who interviews people, I have seen thousands of résumés. However, I can count on one hand the number of truly exceptional résumés that have crossed my desk. Sadly, this included more than a few gifted people camouflaged by their own unfocused presentation. On paper, they looked just like everybody else.

I could bore you with statistics about how long the average interviewer spends reading a résumé, but I won't. Believe me, it's not long. Although it's likely that every word of your cover letter will be read, the same cannot be said of your résumé.

Individuality, as it relates to the résumé, is not a synonym for creativity. Rather, it is the degree to which the résumé positions the candidate as both unique and qualified.

Upon first seeing the résumé, the reader should think: *there is no one in the world this could be except you.*

Too often, the assessment can only be: *this could be anybody in the world including you.*

The distance test One of the most effective ways to gain insight into the interviewer's perspective is through the distance test. If you have already written a résumé, use it for this exercise. (Otherwise, photocopy the sample "skeleton" and "cluttered" résumés.) Pin the résumés on the wall and stand back five to seven feet. What can you read?

Unless your eyes are exceptionally strong, you will only be able to read the name, the category headings, and possibly a company name or two. What does that say? If it's your résumé, it says that where you worked is more important than what you did. For your sake, I hope that's not true.

If you think of the résumé as a one-page ad for you, it makes sense that you wouldn't want the most prominent communication to be "Experience," "Education," and "References available on request."

Contentwise, the skeleton résumé and the cluttered résumé represent opposite extremes, but their similarities are more striking; they are both hopelessly unfocused and sadly typical.

The skeleton résumé The first sample is a "skeleton" résumé in the sense that it is short on specifics. Without focus and personality, it could literally belong to anyone. The capitalization, the boldface type, the type size, and the white space that surrounds them make the category headings the most prominent elements. However, in their existing generic state, they represent unrealized potential.

In the unlikely event that a recruiter were to spend more than a few seconds reading this résumé, he or she would be struck by the difference between the actual communication and what was probably intended. This issue could be addressed with headings that are both active and skill-focused. "Experience" is neither. Countless people passively experience life. Far fewer make the most of their opportunities.

The fact that Emery chose to subdivide "experience" into "related" and "other" creates further confusion. Theoretically, each point under "related experience" is relevant to the employer. But how? Emery has unintentionally placed the onus on the interviewer to determine how each experience is related. Taking this one step further, "other experience" can only be interpreted as "irrelevant." While this was clearly not intended, the objective remains a mystery. This may have been an attempt to demonstrate other areas of responsibility and achievement. Perhaps she was trying to appear well-rounded. Regardless of her intentions, résumés should answer questions, not raise them.

The cluttered résumé The cluttered résumé may lack focus, but it definitely isn't short on detail. In this case, the detail is so overwhelming that it actually prevents the reader from gaining an appreciation of Emery and her accomplishments. Excessive detail is an interesting problem because it highlights the human tendency to believe that more is better. This, incidentally, is not a belief shared by people who read résumés regularly. A recruiter evaluating this résumé would probably reach the following conclusions:

- Emery doesn't know what I need.
- She doesn't know what she has to offer.
- She doesn't respect my time.

As you weigh the relative merits of your experience, keep in mind that job hunting is no different than trying out for a team. If you were competing for a spot on the tennis team, your ability to swim the 100-yard butterfly in Olympic-qualifying time would be irrelevant. You would have to convince the coach that this skill made you a better tennis player. In the same way, a résumé cluttered with meaningless detail does not effectively communicate potential.

The Skeleton Résumé

Emery Stephanie McTell
25 Ocean View Drive
Anytown, USA
(612) 555-1045

EDUCATION STATE UNIVERSITY
B.A. Mass Communications (June 2002)
Minor/Psychology

RELEVANT Consumer Behavior Public Speaking
COURSES Creative Writing Economics
Accounting
Statistics

RELATED STATE UNIVERSITY MARKETING CLUB
EXPERIENCE *President* (1999–2001)
• Led weekly meeting
• Organized campus activities
• Liaison to local businesses and speakers
Member (1998–Present)

SPARE TIME PROMOTIONS (1997–Present)
Sold jewelry and other arts/crafts items to local stores

OTHER JUST FOR FUN DESIGNS (1996–1998)
EXPERIENCE Started business designing and manufacturing jewelry

ACTIVITIES SPECIAL OLYMPICS (1995–Present)
Volunteer Coach
UNIVERSITY NEWS (1999–Present)
Marketing Columnist
WAVO-FM (Student Radio Station) (2000–Present)
Disc Jockey, Newscaster

	TENNIS TEAM (State University) Member	(1998–Present)
HONORS & AWARDS	1999 Distinguished Young Business Person (Anytown Chamber of Commerce) Dean's List President's Scholarship	
COMPUTER EXPERIENCE	Proficient in Microsoft Word, Harvard Graphics, Charisma, Lotus, Pro A/R, Adobe Desktop Publishing, and Quickbooks. Seasoned Web surfer.	

Your life on one or two pages

A résumé is not a summary of your experience as dictated by a standard format that includes headings labeled Name, Objective, Education, and Experience. A résumé is your life, on one or two pages, as it relates to the position you are pursuing. It is also a reflection of the person you are becoming. After reviewing your cover letter and résumé, the reader should be convinced that the position you're pursuing is a logical next step in your development. In this sense, an effective résumé is a synthesis of the insights gained through the self-analysis and target analysis (Chapters 2 and 3). A recruiter should be able to glance at the résumé and think: This person knows what I am looking for in an employee. There is definite potential here.

What not to include

To make room on the résumé for specific, relevant, and quantified experience, we will first review those facts that can be excluded. This includes objectives, references, and grade point averages. Although some recruiters disagree, I feel strongly that this information does not belong on a résumé.

Objectives/references A clearly stated objective belongs in the cover letter, not the résumé. It isn't necessary or helpful to include flowery, meaningless detail about a "challenging position" at a "progressive company" that "utilizes your organizational skills, attention to detail, and ability to work with people." Sound familiar? I have seen the same objective—stated more or less verbosely—and have never been

The Cluttered Résumé

Emery Stephanie McTell
25 Ocean View Drive
Anytown, USA
(612) 555-1045

EDUCATION   STATE UNIVERSITY
B.A. Mass Communications   (June 2002)
Minor/Psychology
Funded over 65% of tuition/spending money through
part-time business ventures.

EXPERIENCE   STATE UNIVERSITY MARKETING CLUB
President   (1999–2001)
Led weekly meetings • Organized campus activities •
Secured marketing agreements with local businesses •
Designed and monitored work/study programs •
Developed business/marketing plans for local
entrepreneurs and other small start-up companies •
Worked with University to arrange academic credit for
special club projects • Booked speakers (e.g., local
business owners, advertising executives) • Created campus
events to boost club awareness/participation •
Represented club to student finance committee •
Identified faculty sponsors for the club.

JUST FOR FUN DESIGNS   (1989–Present)
Designed and manufactured a line of custom jewelry,
accessories, and greeting cards • Maintained database of
customers for holiday direct mail program • Sold items
through local stores • Managed all aspects of the business
including accounts receivable, retail support, direct
marketing, inventory, and sales.

SPARE TIME PROMOTIONS   (1997–Present)
Represented myself as well as other local artists, entrepreneurs, and craftspeople • Built extensive network of contacts including over 15 local businesses and 30 artisans • Donated portion of proceeds to "Young Artists At Risk"—an art program for lower income children • Recruited and coordinated high school and college students to create awareness and interest in *SPARE TIME* goods • Set prices • Determined profit/loss projections.

ACTIVITIES

UNIVERSITY NEWS (Marketing Columnist)   (1999–Present)
Conceived and wrote a weekly column covering the activities of various student business organizations including the *State University Marketing Club* • Recruited club members and local business owners to appear as guest columnists.

WAVO-F (Student Radio Station)   (2000–Present)
Disc Jockey, Newscaster • Hosted Friday evening new music feature • Created station promo tapes and Public Service Announcements • Prepared and announced Monday evening news.

TENNIS TEAM (State University)   (1998–Present)

HONORS & AWARDS

1994 Distinguished Young Business Person Award (Anytown Chamber of Commerce), voted 1994 Best Columnist/University News, Dean's List (3 years), Presidential Scholarship, 2000 Who's Who in American College Students, Special Olympics Coach (6 years).

COMPUTER EXPERIENCE

Proficient in Microsoft Word, Harvard Graphics, Charisma, Lotus, Pro/AR, Adobe Desktop Publishing and QuickBooks. Seasoned Web surfer.

impressed. If you feel compelled to put an objective on the résumé, limit it to a phrase like "investment banking," "occupational therapy," "brand management," or "public relations" that is relevant to the industry.

"References available upon request" is another urge you should resist because it's a given. If and when potential employers want references, they will ask for them. They assume you've got references, so there's no point in telling them what they already know.

Grade point average (GPA)

In the spirit of full disclosure, whether the GPA should be included is an area where I differ from many recruiters. For some, GPA is important as an indicator of intelligence, motivation, and the ability to set and achieve goals. Thus, the absence of a GPA raises questions.

I view it differently. If your résumé is focused and truly speaks to the company's needs, the fact that you didn't include a GPA will probably not eliminate you from consideration. Interviewers who are that interested (or narrow-minded) will ask anyway. I, on the other hand, don't care how you were graded; I want to know what you learned. I want to know whether you have the personality, the leadership ability, and the common sense to succeed. I want to know if you'll do well on my team. No grade can ever tell me that.

For all but a select few, a stellar GPA represents years of hard work and sacrifice. However, unless you are also applying to medical school, there is no tangible benefit to earning a 4.0. Furthermore, there can be a price for emphasizing your GPA. You might have to work harder to convince a prospective employer that you're active and involved in nonacademic activities. As the interviewer, I would also probe deeper on your ability to handle difficult people and uncomfortable situations. If you are truly multidimensional, creative, interesting, and in touch with the world, you won't have trouble convincing me—but we'll waste time getting there.

In my own case, I did not include a GPA on my résumé. Only one inexperienced person ever cared enough to ask. While almost no interviewers asked about my grades, a few insightful people did ask what I learned and in which subjects I excelled. This is because most experienced interviewers are aware that life's most valuable lessons are rarely taught in the library.

What to keep short and sweet

Computer literacy

Within our lifetime, I fully expect that this category will become unnecessary as it relates to basic word processing and spreadsheet skills. Until then, its absence raises questions. Unless the company has specific requirements such as extensive Internet experience, by stating that you are computer literate, you'll cover all the bases.

Of course, if you're pursuing a career with an Internet or computer-related company, you will need to be more specific about the software and programming languages with which you have proficiency. Some Internet companies, for example, look for Web programmers who are comfortable with Java, C++, and other programming languages. Likewise, many graphic design firms look for candidates who are skilled with QuarkExpress, Photoshop, and Illustrator. In any case, just make sure you highlight whatever expertise is relevant. The key is knowing what is relevant: Take the time to find out, and you'll start out well ahead of your competition.

Building Your Résumé

Now that you've gone through an exhaustive inventory of your personal assets and liabilities and seen some of the common pitfalls to avoid, it's time to match your skills with the needs of potential employers. On a separate sheet of paper for each company that interests you, list the required, company-specific skills such as leadership, problem solving, and strategic thinking. These qualities will be the focus of both your cover letter and résumé. Using your notes from the questions above, as well as the information from your self-analysis, list the experiences that demonstrate your abil-

ity and potential. Think beyond job titles to actual accomplishments.

Quantifying your experience

Whenever possible, the experiences on your résumé should be focused on results and quantifiable. Unfortunately, this is where most people fall apart because they haven't taken the time to make clear the exact nature of their contributions. The more specific you can be about the impact you've made, the more believable and convincing it will be. Don't worry about conveying the appearance of bragging. As long as you stick with the facts, it won't be considered bragging.

Consider the difference between the following entries:

> **General experience:** *Organized fund-raising efforts for the Leukemia Research Foundation (1990)*

> **Quantified/results-oriented experience:** *Created and organized direct-mail fund-raising effort that yielded a record 35 percent participation and an additional $750,000 for bone marrow transplants (Leukemia Research Foundation, 1990)*

Both of the entries communicate that the person organized fund-raising efforts. However, in the first entry, the extent of the effort is not at all clear. The "fund-raising efforts" may have been limited to convincing a little brother to knock on a neighbor's door requesting a donation. It's also possible that months of effort, hard work, rejection, and eventual success are camouflaged behind "organized fund-raising efforts." Given this entry, there's no way to know. That's why it's so important to quantify your efforts. Otherwise, you'll miss a valuable opportunity to convince a potential employer of your ability and potential. Unfortunately, most people never communicate the exact nature of their contributions on résumés or even in interviews.

At first it might seem odd that fabulous results would be more believable than a generic "organized fund-raising efforts," but it often works out that way. To a prospective employer, nonspecific entries like the first one above are often assumed to be fluff. After all, it's common knowledge that people include activities in which they are only peripherally involved to appear more well-rounded or better qualified. Therefore, anyone who takes the time to quantify his or her accomplishments is generally assumed to have been involved in a significant way.

In addition to highlighting the results, the second entry is clearly superior because it communicates initiative. The fact that this person created the direct mail fund-raising effort makes it clear that this was a new program. Creating and implementing programs takes initiative. When other people are involved in the effort, new programs like this also require leadership. Thus, to better communicate the scope of the project, the entry might be revised as follows:

Led team of ten in creation and execution of direct-mail fund-raising effort to 100,000 local residents. Campaign yielded a record 35 percent response rate and an additional $750,000 for bone marrow transplants (Leukemia Research Foundation, 1990)

Once you've taken the time to quantify your experiences, you will be in a much better position to sell yourself on paper and in an interview. By making this effort, you'll be more attractive to a potential employer than most of your competitors, who will never take the time to do this. That's exactly the advantage you need to get the job you want. For another look at the power and insight that can come from quantifying your experiences, read the "Concert Violinist Seeks Marketing Position" case study.

Outside interests/life experiences

An insightful interviewer can learn a lot from a person's interests and experiences. Assuming that your résumé already speaks to the needs of a particular company, this may be the most important category you include. It might sound strange, but this could ultimately be what distinguishes you from the competition. This category answers four important questions:

- What makes you special?
- Have you had any unique experiences?

- How do you spend your free time?
- What do your outside interests reveal about you?

My favorite example of including outside experiences was done by my friend Jerry Dow. His last entry captured his personality in a simple, yet memorable way:

A Little Bit More

I have also: hauled hay, pumped gas, mixed chemicals, plowed fields, waited tables, worked in a gun shop, worked in a machine shop, worked in the oil fields, photographed birthday parties, tended bar, milked a cow, saved a life, jumped from an airplane, and met Jerry Lewis.

This makes it clear that Jerry values every moment of his life. It is also revealing that he would write "milked a cow" and ten other phrases before "saved a life." It strongly suggests that Jerry is a down-to-earth person who doesn't arrogantly view himself as a hero. Not surprisingly, "A Little Bit More" inspired most of the résumé-related questions that came up in Jerry's interviews. My own résumé includes an entry that was effective for a number of different reasons:

What Makes Me Smile

Teaching preschool
Volunteering (Children's Memorial Hospital, 1984–present)
Piano, guitar, trombone, & voice lessons
CD/record collecting

Improvisation (Second City Player's Workshop)
Stock & options trading
Skydiving
Scuba diving (Advanced/Rescue)
Springboard diving
Weight-training
Art collecting
Reiki (Level II)
Yoga

At least three-fourths of the questions generated by my résumé came from this category. Without exception, the interviewers wanted to learn more about my involvement in whatever area happened to interest them.

When I earned my Open Water Certification for scuba diving, I added it to the list. Of my next four interviews, three were with certified divers. The fourth planned to take classes. How do I know? Before we even sat down, each interviewer asked, "So, where have you been diving?" As fellow divers, we bonded instantly. As an interviewee, there's no better feeling (except, perhaps, a job offer).

The personal touch— on résumés

There are certain questions that seem to come up repeatedly concerning résumés. One of the most common sources of confusion is whether to include personal interests. I differ with many of the traditional career experts on this question because I don't believe a single answer or course of action

Concert Violinist Seeks Marketing Position

Not long ago, I was approached by a concert violinist who wanted help getting a job in advertising. Not surprisingly, her three-page résumé focused almost exclusively on her experience as a violinist. I was confused and challenged. First, I had a hard time understanding why a violinist who played with Sir Georg Solti, Daniel Barenboim, and the Moody Blues would make the switch to advertising. Second, assuming her passion for advertising was genuine, how could she possibly position twenty years of orchestral experience to make it clear that account management was the next logical step? How could she position this on a résumé?

Answers to these questions became apparent only after I challenged her to chart the accomplishments in every area of her life. My questions and instructions were as follows:

- Under what circumstances have you been recognized by others?
- In what areas have you earned additional responsibility?
- How did you get involved in teaching? Did students find you or did you find them?
- How many students have you taught?
- How much did you charge? How have your rates changed?

When she returned with fifteen pages of notes, I noticed underlying themes of marketing and leadership in almost every area of her life. Suddenly I understood her interest in account management. She was recognized as a leader at age twelve when she began teaching violin lessons at the music school's request. From there, she marketed herself as a teacher, classroom instructor, musician, and manager of a string quartet. As she described the various marketing challenges, a more focused, enthusiastic person emerged.

We applied this insight to her other experiences with similar results. Even as a temp at a high-end equipment manufacturer, she had established a record of achievement, recognition, and additional responsibility. Examples of strategic thinking and problem solving emerged from each experience. Until that point, her cover letter, résumé—even her interviewing style—positioned her as a concert violinist who suddenly wanted to pursue advertising. Now, her positioning matches her achievements:

She is an accomplished marketer, problem-solver, and strategic thinker— who also happens to be a concert violinist.

can be used every time. It truly depends. While many recruiters insist that personal interests are irrelevant, I'm a strong believer that they can be used effectively. I've done it myself, and I've coached countless people in using personal interests successfully. The only safe strategy is to do your homework. Ask yourself:

- What are you communicating?
- Why should a recruiter care?

As you might imagine, facts such as your age, marital status, race, religion, and birth weight do not belong on the résumé. But that's not usually the problem. More often than not, the uncertainty arises around hobbies, interests, and experiences. To resolve the issue, it's important to make a few distinctions.

For many, the word "hobbies" conjures up images of self-absorbed, purposeless play. To a top accounting firm, details about an applicant's paper clip collection aren't particularly helpful or revealing. In this case, there are two reasons for the irrelevance. First, paper clip collecting won't communicate much to the recruiter unless it somehow enhances a job-related skill. Clearly, that would be a stretch.

The second reason is industry-specific. Top accounting firms, investment bankers (to a lesser extent), and other quant-jocks represent a unique subset of the recruiting population. These number crunchers are not typically good team players. Nor do they have to be. If I'm recruiting for a top accounting firm, I care more about a person's ability to work intelligently, efficiently, and for long hours—often alone. I don't care if he or she would make a great tennis partner or an interesting conversationalist. After all, the more time the person spends playing tennis, participating in or talking about his or her hobbies, the less time there is to make money for me.

In other words, the ideal candidate is a workaholic with no life. And workaholics can work anywhere. I don't have to worry about sending them to West Zanzibar for weeks at a time, because I know they won't be missing anything. Just ask anyone who has worked for one of the top consulting firms. He or she probably didn't even need an apartment—just a toothbrush and a laundry service.

At this point, you might be wondering when a personal interest or experience is relevant, and to whom. This is where I make the distinction between hobbies and experiences. Scuba diving, rock climbing, whitewater rafting, and Outward Bound excursions are just a few of the experiences and interests that extend well beyond what might have once been considered a hobby. In each case, the activity is both social and team-oriented, and it displays a commitment beyond passing interest. People who aren't good team players or who have trouble trusting and working with others don't generally have much interest or ability in these areas. This is relevant to any career that involves teamwork, communication, idea generation, cooperation, client contact, and social interaction. Having spent a year at the Chicago Board of Trade, I can assure you that these qualities are important to almost everyone, even options traders who work together to manage a position.

Personal experiences, passions, interests, and work experience—when viewed as a whole—can provide an insightful interviewer with a fairly accurate understanding of the person behind the résumé. To a thoughtful person, this is important. The world is full of people who can handle the basics of any given job. But I'm willing to bet you wouldn't want to work with most of them.

Establishing a clear timeline

Your experience—from the perspective of the company's needs—may not be consistent with a chronological presentation. If so, don't leave it up to the interviewer to recreate the sequence of events. To avoid fielding a never-ending array of chronological questions, it's often worth taking the time to put a brief timeline on the bottom of the résumé if it appears there are gaps.

If there is a significant period of time you haven't accounted for, address it in the cover letter. As odd as it might seem, this can be a strong selling point. One candidate even used what he learned by failing and having to drop out of college to demonstrate growth, honesty, and maturity. From the perspective of an objective observer, this candidate explained what the experience taught him, how he found focus, and his decision to return to pursue a master's degree. When he finished, there was no trace of the designated drinker who failed out of college. Instead there was a portrait of a determined young man who found wisdom through unconventional means.

When the exact chronology of the résumé isn't apparent, it raises questions:

Has this person accounted for all of his or her time since college?

As an interviewer, gaps and "missing" time on résumés don't concern me unless it's obvious the person is hiding something. For some other recruiters, finding gaps is an obsession that borders on the pathological. It's almost as if these interviewers assume you spent the unaccounted for time in a maximum security prison. Unfortunately, the prevalence of this attitude does little more than induce fear in people who suddenly feel they have to apologize for not working during the two months they spent bike riding to raise money for cancer research.

Are there extended periods of unemployment (or underemployment)?

One of the best ways to avoid this trap is to use years as the dates on your résumé. For example, if you worked in one job from March 1997 to February 1999, battled unemployment for ten months and finally landed a job in December 1999, the dates for the first job would be listed as 1997-1999. Your new job would then be listed as 1999-present. No one needs to know you were unemployed for almost a year. It's just not that important. People who get lengthy severance packages often take the same amount of time to travel. There's not much difference.

If you spent time in a job that doesn't seem to make sense or appears to be a step back from where you were, take the time to explain that in your cover letter. For example, after a layoff, you might have been forced to accept a lower position to pay your bills while you looked for something better. While not ideal, this is perfectly understandable—especially if you have a family to feed.

Has this person made a series of sideways career moves that might

indicate a performance or motivation problem?

It also happens that people who switch companies within the same industry may find themselves with a lower title at a bigger company. When this is the case, explain it in the cover letter by pointing out the greater opportunities at the new company. If you got a raise to join the new company, that would be worth mentioning as well. If you didn't get a raise, don't mention it. There's nothing wrong with a sideways move, or even a step back, if it puts you on a better career path.

There are a number of good reasons people make lateral or seemingly downward career moves, including layoffs, career changes, and relocation. In certain circumstances it may also make sense to take a step back in title when moving from a small company to a large one if a lateral move would have resulted in overwhelming additional responsibility. It may even be that your spouse was transferred to a different city and the only available opportunity was at a lower level than your previous position. In any event, if you made a lateral or downward move, it probably made sense at the time. All you have to do is explain your reasoning in the cover letter or interview.

Establishing a clear chain of events is also important if you've changed jobs frequently within a relatively short period. Let's imagine, for example, that you had five different jobs in five years. To keep employers from reaching unwarranted conclusions about your stability or your ability to get along with people, it's helpful to include under each entry on the résumé a brief explanation as to why you left:

Company 1 (1996)
Reason for leaving: Recruited by Company 2 to start new Indianapolis division.

Company 2 (1997)
Reason for leaving: Corporate restructuring, 10,000 people laid off.

Company 3 (1998)
Reason for leaving: Corporate restructuring. Our entire department was eliminated.

Company 4 (1999)
Reason for leaving: Opportunity to join Company 5, a start-up Internet company. Granted significant stock options.

Company 5 (2000)
Reason for leaving: Unable to attract second wave of venture capital, our company went out of business.

Without listing a reason for leaving, all any potential employer would know is that you held five jobs in five years. By including a brief sentence or two that explains the movement between jobs, it is clear that you are not unstable at all. You didn't voluntarily bounce between jobs. In one case, the firm that hired you actively recruited you. That, by itself, is a strong selling point because it suggests you have a solid professional reputation. In the other cases, you didn't leave because you were bored or having personal issues. Instead, corporate restructuring issues dictated your departure. That's nothing to be ashamed about, because layoffs, unfortunately, are a fact of life.

Now, let's imagine that you held five completely unrelated jobs in five years as you attempted to find yourself. In this case, a potential employer might be justifiably hesitant to hire you for fear that you would leave after they invested time and money to train you. To defuse this fear, you will have to be very convincing about why the particular position is the next logical step in your personal and professional development. At the same time, you'll have to acknowledge your previous instability, accept responsibility for any mistakes you made, and paint a clear picture of the lessons you learned and that will keep you from making those same mistakes again.

Adjusting Your Résumé to Meet Different Needs

In the rest of this section we'll take the detail of the cluttered résumé and apply it to hypothetical account management positions at Agency A and Agency B. We will continue to use Emery McTell, our fictitious candidate, as a model for how someone might pursue these different opportunities.

Although both agencies seek energetic self-starters who possess excellent communications skills (written and verbal), the other entry-level requirements differ, as do the corporate cultures at the two agencies.

The companies

Agency A This is a conservative agency with conservative clients. Account people who excel in this environment would be described as:

- Leaders
- Strategic thinkers
- Problem solvers
- Risk-averse
- Persuasive

Agency B This is a younger agency with more progressive clients. To manage the rapidly changing businesses of its clients, Agency B seeks account people who are:

- Entrepreneurial
- Adventurous
- Creative
- Intuitive
- Resourceful

Respecting your personal preferences

The differences between the agencies raise two questions. First, can Emery market herself for both positions? Second, and more important, *should* Emery market herself for both positions?

As long as Emery takes the time to position herself appropriately, there is no doubt she could compete for both. She could probably even excel at either agency. However, her ability to do the work is not a good predictor of long-term professional satisfaction.

Emery must know herself well enough to know which environment better suits her personality.

The corporate culture at Agency A might be so rigid that Agency B's top performers would feel stifled. Likewise, Agency A's top performers might be so methodical and process-oriented that they lack the entrepreneurial spirit needed to flourish at Agency B.

To make an informed decision, Emery must be aware of these differences. It may be that she is more adventurous than risk-averse. Or perhaps she's more creative than strategic. If either is true, she would probably be happier at Agency B. For the same reasons, it would be in Emery's best interest to focus her job search efforts on other creative, entrepreneurial agencies.

When you find yourself weighing the relative merits of different corporate environments, trust your instincts. You should know whether you're flexible enough to succeed in different work situations. Just remember, the perfect job is not the one your parents want you to pursue. And it may not be the one everyone else wants. There is no perfect job—only the one that's best for you.

Tailoring the résumé

Let's assume that Emery could be happy in either job. In her résumé, she must position her experience to make it relevant for each agency, since it would be a mistake for her to use the same approach for both.

Consider what would happen if Emery sent both agencies a cover letter and résumé that positioned her as creative, adventurous, and entrepreneurial. At Agency B, this approach could generate interest. At Agency A, it would be meaningless and possibly even detrimental.

The résumés on the following pages are approaches that Emery might consider. The first is tailored toward Agency A and the second is more appropriate for Agency B. Although the focus differs, the communication in both is accurate, honest, and relevant.

The conservative company

To address the needs of Agency A, Emery focuses on leadership, strategic thinking, persuasiveness, and those aspects of her experience that best support her potential. Even the headings (Marketing, Writing & Presentations Skills) fit the company's needs.

The progressive company

For Agency B, Emery's challenge is to create a résumé featuring the entrepreneurial spirit, adventurousness, creativity, intuitiveness, and resourcefulness that Agency B seeks in entry-level employees.

Emery focuses on her experience as a marketing columnist because she used it as a free publicity vehicle for the marketing club. It is a great example of resourcefulness. The mileage Emery gets from this exceeds what she could have achieved using her leadership experience as the marketing club representative, her marketing experience in creating a customer database for Spare Time Promotions, or her business-generating public relations article for Just For Fun Designs—none of which were included in this version of her résumé.

As you can see, creating an effective résumé is an art rather than a science. To improve your chances, seek informational interviews. Request feedback. Look for ideas everywhere. However, don't worry about getting consensus about your presentation. Just make sure you've taken the time to understand the needs of the company, for then you will be in a much better position to highlight the experiences that demonstrate your potential most convincingly. And remember, you will never have a "final" product. You will evolve, and so should your résumé.

Job changes versus career changes

No matter what study you read, it's apparent that people today are likely to change careers at least once during their working life. Others tend to change careers even more often. Whatever the circumstances, changing careers presents a special challenge from a job-hunting perspective.

The difference between a job change and a career change is relatively straightforward. Changing jobs involves moving from one company to another within the same industry.

A career change, on the other hand, involves moving from one industry to another. If a physical therapist decides to pursue a position with an exercise equipment manufacturer, that would be considered a career change, even though there are certain synergies between the two careers.

Depending on the position, the physical therapist's understanding of physiology would probably be valuable to the exercise equipment manufacturer. Nevertheless, the shift would still be considered a career change.

From a job-hunting perspective, the career change is more challenging because it involves repositioning yourself for a career in which you may have no formal experience. What makes it even more difficult is that employers are often predisposed to hiring people with experience in their industry. Your challenge is to convince them you're worth the risk. Better still, your reasons for changing careers should be crystal clear. Find a way to position your desired career as the next logical step in your professional development. Since it's easier to make the case in a letter, you will find the cover letter is a more important tool than the résumé.

When I decided to change careers from advertising to options trading, my résumé didn't come close to telling the story. From a job perspective, I had never been hired to anything related to trading. Any employer looking solely at my résumé would probably have thrown it away. But that didn't happen. Instead, I took the time to craft a convincing cover letter describing the origin of my interest in trading.

I explained that I had become interested in trading at a young age because my grandfather was a soybean trader at the Chicago Board of Trade. With his encouragement, I began studying the markets, bought my first stock at age ten and continued investing throughout my life. At the same time, I became interested in options and independently studied the topic.

By tracing my interest and demonstrating what I had learned on my own, I convinced several options trading firms to grant me an interview. From there, it was easier to demonstrate that my interest wasn't just something that developed overnight.

To further illustrate the importance of tailoring your presentation, I have included examples of my own résumé on the following pages. The "Marketing Résumé" gives a general idea how I might summarize my experiences for a marketing-related position. This, however, would not be an effective résumé for the freelance writing jobs I have pursued more recently. That's why I created a completely different résumé for writing jobs.

Having gone through the hard work of putting together a résumé, it's essential to put the same effort into constructing a well-written, convincing cover letter. Otherwise, your résumé might never make it into the right person's hands. In the next chapter, we'll examine the essential ingredients in a cover letter that will give you the best shot at getting the interview.

Sample Résumé: Agency A

Emery Stephanie McTell
25 Ocean View Drive
Anytown, USA
(612) 555-1045
email: emctell@xxx.edu

EDUCATION   STATE UNIVERSITY
B.A. Mass Communications; Minor/Psychology   (June 2002)
Computer Literate

MARKETING   MARKETING CLUB PRESIDENT (STATE UNIVERSITY)
Elected for 3 terms   (1999–2001)
Leadership/Team Skills
> Became youngest club president (elected unanimously
> as a sophomore) • Championed club restructuring •
> Recruited faculty sponsors • Designed club projects
> with local businesses/entrepreneurs • Represented club
> to university finance committee.

Persuasion/Motivation
> Convinced school to award academic credit for club
> projects/internships • Increased active club
> membership from 15 to 105 • Attracted 20 new
> businesses for campus recruiting (12 of these firms
> then hired 17 seniors over a 2 year period).

FOUNDER & MARKETING REPRESENTATIVE   (1997–Present)
SPARE TIME PROMOTIONS
Leadership
> Represented local artists/craftspeople to area
> businesses • Generated $2,500.00 per month in sales
> after 3 years • Recruited, trained, and coordinated high
> school and college students to create awareness and
> interest in *Spare Time* products.

Strategic Planning
> Built extensive network of contacts including over 15 local businesses and 30 artisans • Created customer database • Designed/implemented 3 direct marketing promotions which generated sales increases of 30%, 35%, and 45%.

FOUNDER, MARKETER & DESIGNER (1996–1998)
JUST FOR FUN DESIGNS
Marketing & Public Relations
> Designed/created custom jewelry • Sold items through local stores • Generated awareness/new business by writing feature article on *Just For Fun Designs* that ran in local paper. Results: Expanded distribution to 3 new retail outlets • 15% sales increase • Five local artists who read the article requested marketing assistance.

WRITING & PRESENTATION SKILLS

MARKETING COLUMNIST (1999–Present)
STATE UNIVERSITY NEWSPAPER

NEWSCASTER/DISC JOCKEY (2000–Present)
WAVO-FM (Student station)

AWARDS

1999 Distinguished Young Business Person Award (Anytown Chamber of Commerce) • Dean's List (3 years) • Presidential Scholarship

INTERESTS

Special Olympics Coach (6 years) • Rock climbing • State University Tennis Team (4 years) • Whitewater rafting • Urban impressionist paintings • Rollerhockey • Agatha Christie books • Yoga

Sample Résumé: Agency B

Emery Stephanie McTell
25 Ocean View Drive
Anytown, USA
(612) 555-1045
email: emctell@xxx.edu

EDUCATION

STATE UNIVERSITY   (June 2002)
B.A. Mass Communications; Minor in Psychology
Computer Literate

MARKETING &
ENTREPRENEURSHIP

MARKETING CLUB PRESIDENT   (1999–2001)
STATE UNIVERSITY
Team Skills/Motivation
Championed club restructuring • Recruited faculty sponsors • Designed club projects with local businesses/entrepreneurs • Convinced school to award academic credit for club projects/internships • Increased active club membership from 15 to 105 • Attracted 20 new businesses for campus recruiting (12 of these firms hired 17 seniors in the past 2 years).

FOUNDER   (1997–Present)
SPARE TIME PROMOTIONS
Initiative
Recognized opportunity to help local artists market their goods/services • Generated $2500.00 per month in sales after 3 years • Self-funded 75% of college tuition/living expenses • Recruited, trained, and coordinated high school and college students to create awareness and interest in *Spare Time* products.

Strategic Planning
>Built network of contacts including over 15 local businesses and 30 artisans • Designed/implemented 3 direct marketing promotions which generated sales increases of 30%, 35%, and 45%.

CREATIVITY & RESOURCEFULNESS

FOUNDER, JEWELRY DESIGNER   (1996–1998)
JUST FOR FUN DESIGNS
>Designed and created custom jewelry • Generated profit of $200 per week by sophomore year of high school.

MARKETING COLUMNIST   (1999–Present)
STATE UNIVERSITY NEWSPAPER
>Conceived/wrote weekly marketing feature to gain free publicity for the Marketing Club and upcoming club projects. Results (within 3 months): Campus awareness of the restructured Marketing Club exceeded 90% • Of new members surveyed, 75% first exposed to the club through the column.

AWARDS

1994 Distinguished Young Business Person Award (Anytown Chamer of Commerce) • Dean's List (3 years) • Presidential Scholarship

OUTSIDE INTERESTS

Special Olympics Coach (6 ys) • Disc Jockey/Newscaster (Student Station) • State University Tennis Team (4 years) • Agatha Christie books • Whitewater rafting • Urban impressionist paintings • Rock climbing • Folk music • Rollerhockey • Yoga

Rob's Marketing Résumé

email: rsullivan@pureplay.com

EXECUTIVE SEARCH

CARPENTER ASSOCIATES, CHICAGO
Retained Executive Search
Vice President, Senior Consultant   (1998–2000)
Senior Consultant (Project Basis)   ongoing
  Clients included Carparts.com, Intuit, Mattel,
  DraftWorldwide, Brierly & Partners, Wunderman,
  Cato Johnson, and others.

ADVERTISING

LEO BURNETT
Account Exec. Asst. AE, CSA   (1990–1994)
Strategic Planning
  McDonald's Food Service: Led Agency team in
  developing marketing plan/creative concepts for
  schools, stadiums, museums, and other alternative
  venues.
Agency-wide
  Initiated and championed agency-wide project to
  computerize print scheduling.
New Product Launch
  Marlboro Medium: Responsible for all facets of one of
  the most successful new product introductions in
  history—over $1 billion sales in first 12 months • Direct
  marketing, research, advertising, promotion, media,
  and POP ($70MM+ budget) • Identified opportunity that
  saved client $250,000 per year in production costs
  without sacrificing quality.
Pro Bono Advertising
  Shedd Aquarium, Chicago: Led Agency team in
  developing consumer/trade advertising.

MARKETING, **WRITING &** ENTREPRENEURSHIP	AUTHOR *Climbing Your Way to the Bottom: Changing the Way You Approach Your Job Search* An approach to job hunting based on the same marketing strategies that generate millions in revenue every day • Contemporary Books recently purchased the rights to this book. It will be revised, expanded, and published as *Getting Your Foot in the Door When You Don't Have a Leg to Stand On* in 2001 • Listed among Top 10 Career Books (*Chicago Tribune*, 7/97) • Used as a textbook by numerous colleges and universities.

PUBLISHING/DIRECT MARKETING
Climbing Your Way . . .

Created/executed profitable direct mail effort to 3,700 university placement directors • Response rate: 3.6%+

CONSULTANT: STRATEGIC BUSINESS DEVELOPMENT (1995)
C Star Systems, Inc.

Immersed myself in previously unfamiliar world of client/server software development • Positioned company and communicated technology via business plan to potential investors.

EDUCATION	NORTHWESTERN UNIVERSITY, Medill School of Journalism M.S. Advertising (June 1990) COLLEGE OF THE HOLY CROSS B.A. Psychology (May 1989)
WHAT MAKES **ME SMILE**	Teaching Preschool • Volunteering (Children's Memorial Hospital, 1984–present) • Scuba (Advanced/Rescue) • Skydiving • Piano, guitar, trombone, voice lessons • Springboard diving • CD/record collecting • Art collecting • Improv with Second City Player's Workshop • Weight-training • Stock & options trading • Yoga • Rieki (Level II)

email: rsullivan@pureplay.com

WRITING & PUBLISHING

AUTHOR

Climbing Your Way to the Bottom: Changing the Way You Approach Your Job Search

> Description: An approach to job hunting based on the same marketing strategies that generate millions in revenue every day. Ideal for people with more potential than experience • NTC/Contemporary recently purchased the rights to this book. It will be revised, expanded, and published as *Getting Your Foot in the Door When You Don't Have a Leg to Stand On* in 2001 • Listed among Top 10 Career Books (*Chicago Tribune*, 7/97) • Used as a textbook by numerous colleges and universities • Endorsed by the American Advertising Federation (AAF) as the top job hunting resource for students interested in careers in advertising.

PUBLISHING/DIRECT MARKETING

Climbing Your Way . . .

> Created/executed profitable direct mail effort to 3,700 university placement directors • Response rate: 3.6%+

FREELANCE WRITING & MARKETING

WEBSITE TUTORIAL

optionsXpress.com

> Created complete tutorial for options trading website.

BUSINESS PLAN WRITING

C Star Systems, Inc.

> Immersed myself in previously unfamiliar world of client/server software development • Positioned company and communicated technology via business plan to potential investors.

SELECTED ARTICLES & PUBLICATIONS	**"THE BRIDGES TO MADISON AVENUE"** *Careers and the College Grad*, Volume 12, No. 1. 1998: 30–32 The editors of this magazine, which is distributed at the Top 50 colleges and universities in the nation, invited me to write this feature article for students interested in advertising.

"GETTING THE SHAFT"
Enter Magazine, Volume 2, Issue 4. July 1997.

"INTRODUCTION"
The AAF Advertising Career Resource Guide, published by the American Advertising Federation Education Services, 1997.
    Invited by the AAF to write Introduction • Quoted extensively throughout the guide.

EXECUTIVE SEARCH	CARPENTER ASSOCIATES, CHICAGO Retained Executive Search Firm	
	Vice President, Senior Consultant	(1998–2000)
	Senior Consultant (Project Basis)	ongoing

    Clients included Carparts.com, Intuit, Mattel, DraftWorldwide, Brierley & Partners, Wunderman, Cato Johnson and others.

ADVERTISING	LEO BURNETT	
	Account Exec. Asst. AE, CSA	(1990–1994)

Strategic Planning
    McDonald's Food Service: Led Agency team in developing marketing plan/creative concepts for schools, stadiums, museums, and other alternative venues.
Agency-wide
    Initiated and championed agency-wide project to computerize print scheduling.

continued

New Product Launch
> Marlboro Medium: Responsible for all facets of one of the most successful new product introductions in history—over $1 billion sales in first 12 months • Direct marketing, research, advertising, promotion, media, and POP ($70MM+ budget) • Identified opportunity that saved client $250,000 per year in production costs without sacrificing quality.

Pro Bono Advertising
> Shedd Aquarium, Chicago: Led Agency team in developing consumer/trade advertising.

TRADING
COOPER NEFF & ASSOCIATES
Options Trader Trainee (1994)
> Worked on the floor of the Chicago Board of Trade in the bond options and futures pits.

EDUCATION
NORTHWESTERN UNIVERSITY, Medill School of Journalism
M.S. Advertising (June 1990)

COLLEGE OF THE HOLY CROSS (May 1989)
B.A. Psychology

WHAT MAKES ME SMILE
Teaching Preschool • Volunteering (Children's Memorial Hospital, 1984–present) • Scuba (Advanced/Rescue) • Skydiving • Piano, guitar, trombone, voice lessons • Springboard diving • CD/record collecting • Art collecting • Improv with Second City Player's Workshop • Weight-training • Stock & options trading • Yoga • Rieki (Level II)

Cover Letters

> I have made this letter longer than usual, because I lack the time to make it short. —*Blaise Pascal*
>
> Not to transmit an experience is to betray it. —*Elie Wiesel*

Judging from the thousands I have read, many people treat cover letters as an afterthought. For these job hunters the cover letter is little more than an obligatory note to accompany a résumé. This is a mistake because the cover letter can be an incredibly valuable selling tool. Time and again I have seen well-written cover letters lead to interviews that otherwise would never have happened. I've also seen cover letters so poorly written that no one ever read the résumé. Because the cover letter is the first thing an employer reads when reviewing a potential candidate, it can either open or close the door to your next job.

A cover letter is neither a professional-looking Post-It note attached to your résumé with the message, "Hey, check this out. I'd really like to work for you," nor an afterthought. Instead, cover letters and résumés work together as distinct parts of the same communication—why an employer needs you more than anyone else.

Unlike your résumé, every word of your cover letter will probably be read. Ideally, it should convince the reader that you are worth interviewing—even before he or she reads the résumé. I also view cover letters as more distinctive and revealing than résumés. A convincing, well-written cover letter will almost always grab my attention because it conveys whether the writer is articulate and intelligent—or at least resourceful enough to seek qualified assistance. In contrast, an ill-conceived, poorly written cover letter makes a powerful negative statement—even when it accompanies a better-than-average résumé.

If you look at the letter below from a strategic standpoint, this approach is closer to begging than marketing. I have seen countless variations of the sample "typical" cover letter. Some use more flowery language, others demonstrate a greater knowledge of the company, but all are equally ineffective because they focus exclusively on what the company can do for the job hunter. It should be the other way around. Recruiters know why they are important to you. What they don't know is why you are important to them.

Now, consider the example of a cover letter that markets the candidate. Unlike the first letter, this letter is highly specific and indicates a good working knowledge of the position, the requirements, and even the employer's educational preferences. Although the writer acknowledges the absence of a preferred degree, there is no apology offered. Instead, the focus remains, as it should, on what the candidate has to offer and how it demonstrates potential. The confidence this conveys is far more convincing

The Typical (and Worthless) Cover Letter

To Whom It May Concern:

Your reputation as the leader in your industry is what attracts me to your company. Further, your training program, considered by many to be the best in the business, would be the ideal place for me to start my career. Although I don't have any formal experience, I just know it would be a perfect fit. All I need is someone to give me a chance. Enclosed is my résumé and contact information. Please call at your convenience to set up an interview. I look forward to hearing from you.

Sincerely,

A Cover Letter That Markets the Candidate

To Whom It May Concern:

I am writing to express my interest in pursuing a position in the Child Life Department of your hospital. When you look at my résumé, you will probably wonder why a former banker would be applying for the position. When I first recognized that the business world was not as fulfilling as I'd hoped, I began the long process of soul-searching. Along the way, I made two important realizations. First, I realized that I'm not driven by money. Indeed, I am ready and willing to accept a lower salary to pursue my passion. Second, I realized that I feel most fulfilled when I am making a difference in the life of a child. As the oldest of seven children—the youngest is fifteen years younger—I've spent most of my life around children. And I've probably changed more diapers than most parents.

Having spent quite a bit of time in the hospital as a child, I also know how it feels to be hospitalized. More recently, as a Child Life Volunteer at a local children's hospital, I gained an even deeper appreciation of the role that Child Life plays in helping young patients and their families cope with hospitalization, prepare for operations, and achieve a relative level of normalcy. Although I don't have a degree in Child Life, I took numerous child development courses as an undergraduate psychology major. While I know you strongly prefer candidates with a degree in Child Life, I am confident that the life experience described above offers strong evidence of my ability to excel in the position. Furthermore, I have already begun exploring the possibility of pursuing the degree at night.

Thank you in advance for your time and consideration. I will call your office next week to see if we can set up an interview. Or, feel free to contact me at your convenience.

Sincerely,

than "I know I'll do a great job. I just need someone to give me a chance"—which, as I noted before, is more like begging.

As you move ahead with your job search, keep the distinction between begging and marketing in mind. When you write a cover letter, write it as if it were your only opportunity to market yourself. Then evaluate what you have written from the point of view of a recruiter. Make sure it communicates potential. If you haven't marketed yourself effectively, don't expect to get an interview. Marketing recruiters, in particular, are unlikely to interview anyone who isn't clear on the concept.

What Is Marketing?

According to Philip Kotler, Professor of Marketing at Northwestern University and noted authority on the subject, marketing is:

> *A social and managerial process by which individuals and groups obtain what they need and want through creating and exchanging products and value with others. From* Marketing Management: Analysis, Planning, Implementation, and Control

"Process" and "exchange" are two of the most important words in this definition. The process typically occurs as a form of communication (e.g., print ad, negotiation, cover letter). Likewise, an exchange can be goods for services, money for services, or money for goods. For an exchange to occur, the buyer and seller must both believe they will be better off having made the exchange.

The same is true in the job market. The process consists of cover letters, résumés, interviews, and any other recruiting tools that enable candidates to market themselves and convince potential employers they are worth hiring. If successful, the process continues with a job offer in which it becomes the company's turn to convince the candidate to accept the job. However, for a job offer to be extended, the employer must be convinced that the company will benefit by having the person on its team. Likewise, before accepting the job the candidate must be convinced that the company will provide an acceptable environment where employees can develop professionally and excel. Until both parties are convinced of the merits of what the other can provide, it doesn't make sense to extend or accept a job offer.

When marketing yourself in a cover letter, you should not force yourself to be creative. Instead, concentrate on answering two basic questions:

- Why am I worth interviewing?
- What do I have to offer?

Too often, candidates focus on the reputation of the company and its resources without regard to the skills they will contribute to the team. Tell employers why they should interview you. You have potential, but you need to demonstrate it. Convince them to give you an interview. Through the following examples and case studies you will see that demonstrating your potential is easier than you might imagine. It takes thought and effort, but with the right preparation, you can do it effectively.

Content

An effective cover letter communicates the following in less than one page:

- Your objective
- Direct comparisons between your skills and the company's needs
- A date you will call to follow up

Your objective

Your reason for writing should be clear within the first few sentences. For example:

> *At the suggestion of our mutual friend Carrie Lederer, I am writing to request an informational interview.*

> *I am writing to express my interest in pursuing an entry-level position in chemical engineering with your firm.*

> *I am writing in response to your recent posting—on the Miami University Career Placement website—for Certified Public Accountants.*

Comparisons between your skills and the company's needs

Before you apply for any position, take the time to learn as much about the company and the position as possible (see Chapter 2). If you are responding to a job posting, read the information carefully before you submit your paperwork. The Internet has made it so incredibly easy to respond to job openings that most people don't take the time to determine if the position is a good match. Instead, that determination is left up to the potential employer. Not a good strategy.

Show that you've done your homework. If you've done the research, you'll know what qualities the company values in whatever position they are seeking to fill. Give specific examples that demonstrate your potential in these areas. It isn't enough to say, "It's great that you are looking for leadership because I am a natural leader." That isn't convincing. Instead, put yourself in the reader's position. Make the person want to meet you. For example:

> *Based on your job description, it's apparent that you need someone with a solid track record of leadership. Just three years after becoming a member, I was unanimously voted president by XYZ's 300 members. Since then I have completed two terms as leader of this organization, which now serves more than 550 members.*

Think of each example in the cover letter as a topic sentence supported by specifics in the résumé. The cover letter makes sense of your experience and relates it to the challenges of the position. The résumé is a reference for those who want more information.

A date you will call to follow up

At the end of your letter, let the person know you will be calling in the next few weeks. For example:

> *I will call your office in two weeks to see if we can set up an interview at your convenience.*

Allow at least ten days before you call. If you're unable to make contact, leave your name and ask the secretary to suggest a time you might call again. If you are particularly difficult to reach, consider getting an answering machine or voice mail. This may be the best $15 (or less) a month you ever spend.

Proofreading

I shouldn't have to mention this, but your letter should be concise, grammatically correct, and convincing. Otherwise, for the good of the planet, it better be biodegradable.

Before you send any business correspondence, it's a good idea to have another person look over your work. SpellCheck is great, but it doesn't catch everything. Just ask my editors.

The Ineffective Cover Letter

Look at the sample ineffective cover letter. Overall, this is a very weak cover letter because Richard fails to provide an objective, or a reason to believe he is worth interviewing. While he demonstrates a good basic knowledge of the company, Richard doesn't make it clear to Mr. Butler, the recipient in human resources, what department should be interested in Richard. As a result, the letter isn't likely to go anywhere other than the nearest recycle bin.

To improve this letter, Richard should be specific about his objective in the first paragraph. He should clearly state the type of position he is applying for, such as product development, field sales, or whatever. Taking this one step further, he would also improve his chances considerably by identifying the appropriate hiring manager and bypassing human resources altogether.

In the second paragraph, Richard should have drawn specific parallels between his potential, his experience or knowledge, and the company's recruiting objectives. The management at Illinois Superconductor doesn't care what kind of opportunity the company would provide for Richard. But they do care about what Richard has to offer the company as a potential employee.

Unfortunately for Richard, he didn't take the time to make that clear. Here again, he can only provide that information if he knows what qualities are valuable to the hiring managers.

Richard's final mistake is leaving it up to the company to follow up. Unless the company specifically indicates that it does not want phone calls, the candidate should always follow up.

Sample Ineffective Cover Letter (No Reason to Believe)

Mr. John Butler
Human Resources
Illinois Superconductor
Mt. Prospect, IL 60056

Dear Mr. Butler:

In this age of parity products and decreasing profits, only companies that stay on the cutting edge of technology can remain competitive. That's why Illinois Superconductor will be so successful.

What attracts me to Illinois Superconductor is the company's commitment to high-temperature superconducting technology as it relates to the cellular market. The successful field tests that the company has performed in partnership with Ameritech, Southwestern Bell, and other base station operators suggest a bright future for the company's technology in general and Spectrum Master Filters in particular. For these reasons, I am confident that Illinois Superconductor would provide a wonderful opportunity for me to work and learn.

Enclosed you will find a copy of my résumé. I look forward to hearing from you.

Sincerely,

Richard Ashton

A Semi-Effective Cover Letter

Now review the sample of a semi-effective cover letter. The general impression this cover letter creates is pretty good. Overall, Monika does a good job explaining who she is, why she is writing, and how she has demonstrated important marketing skills. To Monika's credit, she even took the time to identify a person currently working in the account management department. Since she stated her objective clearly in the first sentence, she would also have made it easy for human resources to forward her paperwork to the appropriate hiring managers.

Monika also demonstrates a good working knowledge of both the company and its recruiting preferences. While she may have mentioned enough relevant experience to get an interview, she would have increased her chances considerably had she taken the time to make direct comparisons between each skill and the company's needs. As it stands, she referenced only her strategic problem-solving skills directly.

Describing how she used the knowledge she gained at the Leukemia Research Foundation to benefit Half Court Press certainly qualifies as an example of initiative, but she would have done well to be more direct in comparing that experience to the company's need. Furthermore, Monika doesn't provide any examples of leadership or communication skills. While she clearly has potential, she isn't as convincing as she could be. As a result, she'll have some work to do in her interviews if and when she gets that far.

Tailoring the Cover Letter

In the previous chapter, we used the experiences of Emery McTell, a fictitious college student, to demonstrate how the same experience can be tailored in a résumé to match the needs of different companies in the same industry. Emery highlighted different skills for Agency A, a conservative company, and Agency B, an entrepreneurial company. Using the principles we've just discussed, we'll now examine how Emery might tailor her cover letters to each company.

What makes Emery's cover letters effective is the combination of her specific, relevant examples and her knowledge of each company and its needs. The same is true for you. If you don't know what the company is looking for and you haven't done a thorough self-assessment, it will be impossible to write an effective cover letter. However, if you've taken the time to understand who you are and why the position is the next logical step in your development, you have a much better shot at convincing a potential employer to bring you in for an interview.

The conservative company

To address the needs of Agency A, Emery focuses on leadership, strategic thinking, persuasiveness, and those aspects of her experience that best support her potential. The cover letter acknowledges these qualities and makes comparisons between Emery's developing skills and the requirements

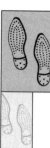

Semi-Effective Cover Letter

Mr. James Tolhurst
Senior Account Executive
Kroll Communications
Chicago, IL 60611

Dear Mr. Tolhurst:

I am writing to express my interest in pursuing a career in account management with Kroll Communications. Enclosed you will find a copy of my résumé for your review.

I understand that you look for individuals who possess initiative, strategic problem-solving abilities, leadership, and strong communication skills. These are skills I have honed through my marketing internships at the Leukemia Research Foundation and Half Court Press.

Recognizing my passion for marketing, a vice president at the Leukemia Research Foundation invited me to participate in the strategic planning and implementation of their direct marketing programs. Later, I applied this knowledge to improve the direct response efforts at Half Court Press. As a result, the company is better able to track consumer purchase behavior. The company is also using this system to monitor the impact of specific marketing efforts at the retail level.

My experience in nonprofit and consumer-oriented marketing is a strong indicator of my potential at a company like Kroll Communications. I am particularly attracted to the company's focus on integrated marketing. The success of The Winnetka Brewery, Grizzly Bear Bottling, and others is a strong testimony to the agency's strength and vision. These are just a few of the reasons I would be proud to contribute my skills to the Kroll team.

I will call you in two weeks to set up an interview at your convenience. Thank you for your time and consideration.

Sincerely,

Monika McMurtry

Sample Cover Letter: Agency A

Ms. Jennifer Alexander
Agency A
Anytown, USA 99999

Dear Ms. Alexander:

I am writing to express my interest in pursuing a career in account management with Agency A. In your presentation at State University last week, you emphasized the Agency's commitment to recruiting persuasive, energetic people who are passionate about marketing. These are just three of the qualities I can offer Agency A.

Over seven years ago, I began designing jewelry as a hobby. Within a few months, I found myself swamped by requests from friends and acquaintances. As demand continued to build, I convinced several local businesses to carry the line under the name "Just For Fun Designs."

Before long, I realized that I enjoyed marketing even more than jewelry design. At that point, I shifted my focus and formed Spare Time Promotions. Through this venture, I used my talents to promote local craftspeople. As the liaison between artists and store owners, I operated much like a traditional account executive. I represented the artists to the stores and the stores to the artists in an ongoing effort to manage the needs and expectations of each.

Later, I used the skills I developed through Spare Time Promotions to lead a team that transformed the Marketing Club at State University. Before the end of the school year, we started working with local businesses on a project basis. As a result, many of these same companies began to recruit at State University.

I would welcome the opportunity to contribute my developing talents to Agency A. I will call you in two weeks to set up a meeting at your convenience.

Thank you very much for your time and consideration.

Sincerely,

Emery McTell

Sample Cover Letter: Agency B

Ms. Amber Overholt
Agency B
Anytown, USA 99999

Dear Ms. Overholt:

While surfing on the Internet, I found a link to your Web page and was truly impressed by what I read. It is refreshing to see an agency so dedicated to entrepreneurial clients that it accepts partial payment in client stock. This vision is what inspired me to explore the possibility of contributing my talents to Agency B.

Over the past seven years, I have experienced the thrill of starting two part-time businesses. In the process, I have begun to develop and nurture many of the qualities that make Agency B successful. Specifically, I have an energetic, entrepreneurial spirit, and I am not afraid to take risks. As President of the State University Marketing Club, I was instrumental in nurturing a spirit of teamwork, competition, and growth. Aside from the talented young people within the organization, the club's most valuable asset is the sign that hangs prominently on our wall:

> *Success is not the absence of failure. Rather, it is the ability to view failure as a possible outcome in any worthwhile pursuit. Those who don't fail aren't taking enough chances.*

When I joined the club as a freshman, I was surprised to see fifteen enthusiastic members who were not yet committed to the possibility the club represented. From my own experiences in high school, I knew we could gain exposure working as free marketing consultants to local businesses.

Within a year, we recruited five active faculty sponsors, identified business partners, and convinced the university to award academic credit for more involved projects/internships. As a result, active membership increased 600 percent.

continued

Like Agency B, the Marketing Club has grown with the companies it serves. In this sense, we have created a partnership between the business leaders of today and tomorrow.

I will call you in two weeks to set up a meeting at your convenience. Thank you in advance for your time and consideration.

Sincerely,

Emery McTell

of account management. Having established her credentials up front, the résumé becomes more of a supporting document that highlights specific, quantifiable accomplishments.

The approach described above also has another, less obvious benefit. Matching her skills to the company's requirements gives Emery an advantage from an interviewing standpoint. By addressing these basic questions first, the interview can be more focused and productive.

The progressive company

For Agency B, Emery's challenge is to create a cover letter that features the entrepreneurial spirit, adventurousness, creativity, intuitiveness, and resourcefulness that this company seeks in entry-level employees. By opening the letter by explaining how she learned about the company, Emery makes it clear she is an adventurous, resourceful per-

son who can navigate her way to interesting opportunities—on and off the Web.

A response to an online posting

In the previous chapter we discussed my reasons for creating separate résumés for marketing and writing opportunities. Now, to demonstrate the importance of tailoring the cover letter, I have included an actual job posting I came across on the Internet along with the cover letter I would use to respond. Since a financial website looking for a promotional writer is a great fit for my background, I wrote a cover letter that addresses—as closely as possible—this very specific job description.

While one could argue that the letter could be shorter, I don't see length as a problem in this case. I decided to make it a little longer because my passion for investing doesn't exactly jump off my résumé. Length isn't necessarily an issue as long as the content is interesting, relevant, and supports the person's potential to excel in the position.

Online Job Posting

Exciting and dynamic new website concept is close to launch. Our well-funded company is seeking full- and part-time copywriters to develop and write descriptive promotional campaigns, wordsmith, review, research, and provide content for the project. The target market is comprised of on-line investors, and the website will explore the psychological aspects of the financial markets, aiming to provide our subscribers with a mental advantage, empowering greater success in their trading.

The successful candidate MUST have:

- *A proven track record of highest quality writing/copy*
- *A consuming fascination, some knowledge/experience for markets, investing, on-line trading*

Also required are general computer skills and knowledge of the Internet, and a willingness to meet publishing deadlines as may be required. Freelance writers are also encouraged to respond!

If you are truly qualified and interested in joining an exciting new company with tremendous upside potential, offering competitive salaries, benefits, and stock options, please E-mail your résumé with samples of your previous work.

Telecommuting is OK. No phone calls, please!

Based on this posting, it is clear that the company is seeking full-time, part-time, and freelance writers who are passionate about ("consuming fascination") the financial markets. It is equally important that applicants possess financial copywriting experience ("proven track record") and samples to show. Reading between the lines, a psychology background and an appreciation of investor behavior would be an added plus, as the website explores the "psychological aspects" of the market.

Despite these specific requirements, I am quite sure the company that posted this was inundated with responses from free-lance writers with no financial experience (writing or investing). Although the company specifically stated that it doesn't want phone calls, there's no doubt in my mind it received many. Through their failure to follow simple directions, many candidates will succeed only in eliminating themselves from consideration. For the rest of us, it becomes a matching game as we compare our backgrounds to the company's requirements.

My response to the online job posting follows. After that, a brief analysis describes each paragraph.

Response to Online Job Posting

Re: Copywriter—Online Publication

Dear _____ :

In response to your ad seeking freelance writers for an online investing site, I am submitting my résumé for consideration. Based on your description, the areas where I can best add value include marketing strategy (e.g., writing and developing promotional campaigns), web content, research, and editing.

My track record of success in writing and marketing started with the four years I spent in account management at Leo Burnett, a large Chicago-based advertising agency. My interest in trading and investing goes back even further. After buying my first stock at the age of ten, I was hooked.

Following in the footsteps of my grandfather, a soybean trader at the Chicago Board of Trade, I left the world of advertising and joined a premier options trading firm in 1994. I spent the next year on the exchange floor in the bond options and futures pits. There is probably no better place to feel the excitement and pulse of the markets than amongst several thousand frenzied traders. From a psychological standpoint, the trading floor also made me realize that the market isn't an unpredictable amorphous being. It is a collection of individuals (and firms) constantly reassessing their positions as they react to a never-ending flow of information.

After leaving the Board of Trade, I spent the next several years writing a book to help career changers and entry-level job hunters market themselves more effectively. Shortly after it was published, the *Chicago Tribune* included the book in its list of the Top 10 Career Books (July 6, 1997). The American Advertising Federation, an educational foundation with local chapters at most colleges and universities, also ranked the book as the top job-hunting resource for students. These are just a few of the endorsements that led to a recent contract with McGraw-Hill to expand and republish the book.

This year, I spent several months writing Web-enabled content for options-Xpress—a start-up Internet brokerage firm catering to options traders. OptionsXpress hired me to create an extensive tutorial describing the many trading strategies available to their clients. The site is scheduled for launch later this year.

Feel free to contact me at your convenience. I'd welcome the opportunity to work with you. In any case, good luck with your endeavor. It sounds like a very exciting project.

Best regards,

Rob Sullivan

First paragraph: How I heard about the job and my objective. Second sentence: Given your needs, here's what I can do for you.

Second paragraph: I trace my track record in writing back to my advertising career since at least some of the writing was marketing-related. I also begin to explain my financial experience since it is separate from my marketing background.

Third paragraph: Here I directly address the company's desire to hire someone who can write about "the psychological aspects of the financial markets" by explaining that my insight came from observations working on the trading floor. I could have mentioned my undergraduate psychology degree, but that didn't seem as relevant, given my experience at the exchange. Had I not worked on the trading floor for a year, I would definitely have mentioned the degree.

Fourth paragraph: I build a case for a "successful track record" by providing endorsements and testimonials so the recipient can see what other people say about my writing. Anytime you can demonstrate that others value your work, do it. It says a lot more than we can believably say about our own work.

Fifth paragraph: My track record is further enhanced by the fact that optionsXpress hired me to do a similar project.

In Search of a Different Drummer

For the next few minutes imagine yourself as a software industry veteran. Over the past eight years you have worked your way up from project coordinator to your current position, International Product Manager at a large computer company. Along the way, the only jobs you have been paid to do were software-related. But now, as your thirty-fourth birthday approaches, you realize your heart isn't in it anymore. Instead, what you really want is to be more involved with promoting and booking bands. All your life you've been passionate about music, but you never pursued it as a career.

Fortunately, the time is right because a Midwestern agency that specializes in representing singer-songwriters is looking to hire another booking agent. However, like so many companies, this one is ideally looking for someone who has already worked in the industry. With a résumé focused on the software industry, what do you do? An impossible challenge? Not for Krista, who found herself in this exact situation.

Read the cover letter below that Krista used to convince the company to interview her for the booking agent position. For Krista, like most career changers, the cover letter is a far more important selling tool than the résumé, because it allows her to explain her background as well as her decision to switch gears at this point in her career.

Dear Talent Agency:

Enclosed is my résumé and supporting information for your consideration for the open booking agent position at your agency. This résumé represents my professional (paid) career, but does not reflect my booking agent and related experience.

For two years (1/96 through 1/98) I booked The Sherpas, comprised of Tom Kimmel, Tom Prasada-Rao, and Michael Lille. I didn't intend for this to be a long-term commitment, but I was so taken with their music and had so much fun, I couldn't help but continue to get them out there! Though The Sherpas have disbanded, I continue to book dates for both Tom Kimmel and Michael Lille on an as-needed basis (neither is touring full-time at present).

As the Sherpas' agent I was responsible for planning regional tours as their schedules permitted. The Sherpas toured in San Francisco, Oklahoma, Kansas, Texas, Alabama, Tennessee, Maryland, Virginia, and D.C. Additionally, The Sherpas appeared in the emerging songwriter showcase at NEFA '97 and in the Elixir Strings showcase at the national Folk Alliance conference in Memphis.

When booking The Sherpas, I planned routings, scheduled with venues, negotiated contracts, created their press kit, sent out press releases, did fan mailings, secured radio interviews, and prepared itineraries and related information for the band. I was part of the team. I staffed tours and conferences, made and distributed demo CDs, and applied for festivals and conferences on The Sherpas' behalf. I was a cheerleader, motivator, sounding board, production coordinator, strategist, advocate, and emissary, and I loved it! I did all this free of charge while holding down a full-time job.

Though I didn't know what I was doing when I started out, I credit my success to the skills I learned from stage-managing theater and project-managing software development. I come by my organizational skills naturally. My professional experience has taught me what it means to be part of a team and how to coordinate and cooperate with others; how to work on a piece of the puzzle without losing sight of the big picture; the importance of enthusiasm and attitude in ensuring success; the value of being a good communicator; how to work under pressure; and how to work across functional boundaries with people who have agendas different from my own.

So why a booking agent at this point in my career? Because I'm passionate about music, and have learned that work is just work if you're not doing something you love. I loved booking The Sherpas. I'm great at putting things together (plays, software, tours). Nothing thrills me more than the thought of applying my passion for music and my organizational and teamwork skills to the business of spreading great music far and wide!

continued

Despite my relative lack of booking experience, I believe that I bring the right skills to the booking agent position, and I hope that this letter conveys my enthusiasm for the job. I look forward to meeting with you in person to further discuss the position and my qualifications.

Sincerely,

Krista

Krista's Technique

To fully appreciate why this letter works for Krista and how any career changer can adapt a similar technique, it's helpful to examine the structure and content of her letter.

After establishing her reason for writing, Krista immediately begins to describe the origin of her interest. This helps her make the case that she has potential beyond what appears on her résumé. Like most career changers, what makes Krista an attractive candidate is not what she has been paid to do, but what she has pursued because of a genuine interest.

As Krista describes her involvement with The Sherpas, her passion, energy, and sincerity come through in every sentence. Better still, she isn't afraid to reveal herself and her true feelings:

> *I didn't intend for this to be a long-term commitment, but I was so taken with their music and had so much fun, I couldn't help but continue to get them out there!*

Not until the end of the fourth paragraph does the reader realize that she didn't charge The Sherpas at all. A true labor of love.

After describing the specifics of how she promoted The Sherpas, Krista wisely takes it one step further and attributes her success to the skills she acquired stage-managing theater and project-managing software development (her full-time job). In this way, Krista convincingly makes the case that music booking is the next logical step in her professional development. Just to be sure, she asks and answers the question directly:

*So why a booking agent at this point in my career? Because I'm passion-
ate about music, and have learned that work is just work if you're not
doing something you love.*

I don't believe I've ever heard it put better or more convincingly.
Not surprisingly, Krista got the interview and the job. Now, she spends
every day doing what she loves.

As you see from the case study "In search of a Different Drummer," the same approach works for career changers who have held positions completely unrelated to their current career goals.

Now that you know how to construct a convincing cover letter to go along with your résumé, it's time to prepare for the interviews that will be coming your way. Over the next two chapters we'll look at exactly what an interview is, the different styles you might encounter, and questions you should be prepared to answer. Once you know what to expect, you'll find that interviews are just two-way conversations that can actually be fun.

Interviews

> Most ignorance is vincible ignorance. We don't know because we don't want to know.
> —*Aldous Huxley*

Given the complexity of the interviewing process, this chapter will be the most comprehensive. It is also potentially the most valuable. My purpose is to present a clear picture of the interview process, starting with a variety of tips and exercises designed to help you prepare. This also includes an in-depth examination of my own interviewing methods as well as other styles you might encounter. As an interviewee, you have the right to know what is expected. At the same time, it is important to recognize that there is more than one way for interviewers to accomplish their objectives. There are as many interview styles as there are interviewers.

Dressing Appropriately

Much has already been written about dressing for interviews, so I won't rehash it here. Whether you are a man or a woman, the bottom line is this: wear a suit—any suit. You can express yourself and have a little flair, just make sure you look professional.

When I was preparing for interviews with Leo Burnett, the career counselors I contacted reminded me that Burnett was a "conservative Midwestern agency where everybody wears a blue pin-striped suit." Before long they had me convinced that I would have to "look the part." Perhaps that's why I hate blue suits to this day. My time would have been better spent learning to relax, because as it turned out, the fashion insight wasn't accurate anyway. Advertising professionals wear every style and color you can imagine. Very rarely did I even wear a suit at Leo Burnett, and today more and more businesses are adopting casual dress codes. Regardless, job applicants should still wear a suit because it conveys respect for the interviewer. It also shows that you have the good sense to dress professionally for important meetings.

As more and more people struggle with allergies, it's a good idea to avoid wearing perfume or cologne to an interview. While you could probably get away with a dab of either, you'd be better off to play it safe and wear none at all. I can think of several interviews where I was so overwhelmed by the candidate's perfume that I found myself with a serious headache within ten or fifteen minutes. These are often the same people who show up with so much makeup that you wonder what they really look like under-neath all that powder and blush. These are not questions you want interviewers to be asking themselves. Furthermore, if the interviewer has difficulty breathing or concentrating, it can't possibly work to your advantage. So do yourself a favor—keep the scent in the bottle.

Videotaped Mock Interviews

Although you can't necessarily see yourself through someone else's eyes, it is possible to view yourself more objectively with the help of a video camera. Once you get past the initial embarrassment, you'll find that the exercise is both illuminating and worth-while. Videotaping is one of the most valu-able services offered by career counseling professionals. If videotaping isn't an option (and it should be), a regular mock interview is still an excellent idea. Either way, this opportunity for practice and constructive criticism will enhance your performance by giving you a deeper appreciation of the per-ceptions you will create with your inter-viewer. You may even be surprised by nervous habits that operate beyond your conscious awareness.

To maximize the benefits of mock inter-viewing, prepare as if it were a real inter-view. Give the mock interviewer all the information you can regarding the company you would like him or her to represent and supply the topics to be covered. (Having done your homework, you have an idea of some of the questions to expect.) After the videotaped session, review the tape twice. First, scan through the tape and listen to the other person's insights. Then, watch the entire interview again and answer the following questions:

An expert is someone who knows some of the worst mistakes that can be made in his subject and how to avoid them. —*Werner Heisenberg*

How concisely and completely did you respond to each question asked?

For most people, answering questions concisely is one of the most difficult challenges. Fortunately, this is also a skill that can be acquired. With practice and concentration, it won't be hard to answer every question in one or two sentences that can be elaborated upon if necessary. This generally requires taking a moment or two to sort your thoughts first.

One strategy you might consider is to practice as if you were going to be interviewed on the five o'clock news. The television interviewer, like the job interviewer, isn't interested in a five-minute preamble. Both want you to get right to the point. For the next few weeks watch news interviews and count the number of questions asked and answered in a two- or three-minute interview and determine how effectively the person being interviewed responded to each. This format provides the best example of the importance of getting straight to the point.

As you will begin to notice, the people who are most impressive on news interviews can give quite a few concise, convincing answers in a two- or three-minute

interview. The least effective people have trouble answering one. How many times have you watched an interview where the person never seemed to get to the point? As a result you, the viewer, begin to lose interest. The same scenario occurs every day in job interviews. The only difference is that it's the interviewer who loses interest when the questions never seem to get answered.

To avoid this trap, make a list of questions that might come up in an interview. Then have a friend ask the questions and time your responses. At first you may be surprised to discover that your answers average several minutes in length. In television terms this means you would have wasted the entire three-minute interview answering one question. Don't let your interviewer share the same pain you feel as a viewer. Practice. Practice. Practice.

The people you see on television who do well in interviews are not necessarily naturally good interviewers. More often than not they became proficient through what people in the industry refer to as "media training." The short, one-sentence answers are referred to as *sound bites*. Media training works because most of the questions in any interview are predictable. Even when they aren't, it's perfectly legitimate to take a brief, quiet moment formulating a response. This is always a better strategy than rambling endlessly toward an answer.

By following this exercise, you will become your own media training expert, therby saving yourself valuable time and money.

How believably did you communicate your strengths?

As you review your videotaped practice interview, do your best to forget that the person being interviewed is you. Instead, view the dialogue critically from the interviewer's point of view. Are your answers convincing and believable? If you took the time to support your strengths with actual examples, then your answers were probably believable; if you spoke in vague generalizations, you probably weren't. In that case, take the time to come up with specific examples that demonstrate your potential.

Did you smile?

When you think about situations or circumstances that bring a smile to your face, interviews probably don't make the list. After all, getting a job is serious business. Nevertheless, it's important to smile. If you have a tendency to come across as too serious, it's even more critical to find a reason to smile in an interview.

If smiling for no reason seems unnatural, find something to smile about. What might that be? Be happy you are being con-

> No matter how dark the world may seem, you have to remember that your own personal worth will eventually shine through if you believe in it. And the best way to keep believing is to smile so much that others think you are the happiest person in the world. Pretty soon, you will be. —*Charlie Mercker*

sidered for a position that would make others envious. Be happy to meet with someone who shares your passion for whatever career you have chosen. Be happy you woke up this morning in a country where you have the freedom to pursue whatever career you choose. Be happy you are healthy and intelligent. Or just be happy.

How might you appear more poised, confident, and convincing?

For the most part, the answer to this question is both subjective and a matter of personal style. It's also a good question to ask of the person who videotaped the mock interview and any friend willing to review the tape.

Are there any nervous tics you need to avoid?

There's nothing better than a videotaped interview to highlight the words we overuse and the twitches we never noticed we had.

Eliminating words, phrases, and fillers like "you know" and "um" is not easy to do. It takes ongoing conscious awareness, but it's worth the effort. One very effective way to become more conscious of these meaningless fillers is to join a public speaking group or class.

For example, Toastmasters International, which has local meetings almost everywhere, has a designated person at every meeting who serves as the "Ah, Um Counter." For each presentation, this person counts the ahs, ums, you-knows, and any other filler words or phrases the speaker might use. There's nothing more humbling than finishing what you thought was a great presentation only to find out you used 8 ahs, 17 ums, and 12 you-knows. Fortunately, becoming conscious of this habit is the first step toward eliminating it and good preparation is the second step.

As you view the videotape, you may be further surprised to notice that you repeatedly squint your eyes, twirl your hair, scratch your nose, or do some equally distracting physical action. It will take some conscious effort to get rid of the nervous tic, but after seeing it on video you will have all the motivation you need to break that habit. It will probably drive you crazier than it did the interviewer.

Assuming you make it through the entire tape without thoroughly beating yourself up, take a few days to reflect on the experience. Then tape another interview and start all over again, because success takes practice.

Informational Interviews

Once you've conducted a few videotaped mock interviews and you're ready to test your skills, start with a few informational interviews. The primary objective of such an interview is to gather knowledge not available from a published source. It is not a substitute for library research because it's not appropriate to waste someone's time looking for factual information you can find on-line or in a book. Instead, treat it as an opportunity to learn how you can position yourself more effectively for a career in the industry. With this information, you can start to get feedback on your own experiences and the degree to which you can use them to convince people of your potential.

Setting up the interviews

Whenever I recommend informational interviews, people almost always ask, "How can I set up an interview when I don't know anyone in the industry?" Good question. First, ask everyone you know if they know anyone who works or ever worked in whatever industry you're targeting. Then go to the placement office at your school or university and get a list of alumni in that field. If that doesn't work, contact any alumni in your area, explain your dilemma, and ask if they know anyone who might be able to help.

The Twenty Second Telephone Interview

As I prepared to make the switch from advertising to options trading, I called the executive vice president of an options firm to set up an informational interview. Having just started to identify my alternatives, I had two objectives: to get feedback on my job search strategy for repositioning myself from advertising to trading, and to ask about other job opportunities within the industry I might consider.

Since I was given the EVP's name by one of his wife's best friends, it never occurred to me that he might not agree to meet. But that's what almost happened. Rather than set up a time, he said abruptly, "Call me in forty-five minutes after the market closes. Then I'll have a minute to see if a meeting is even warranted."

I knew immediately that this was a person who was fiercely protective of his time. Therefore, I would only have a few sentences to convince him that I was worth talking to. For the next half hour I outlined the key points I would have to communicate. When I called back forty-five minutes later, the conversation went something like this:

My grandfather, who was a soybean trader at the Board of Trade, sparked my interest in trading and investing when he helped me buy my first stocks at age ten. It's been my passion ever since. In addition, I have read a number of books on option trading.

Although I've enjoyed advertising, I've decided to pursue trading as a career. More than anything, I don't want to stay put, reach the end of my life, and wonder how things might have been different had I taken the chance.

With that, I heard him take a deep breath. After a pause, he said the words I most wanted to hear: "We really should meet. Can you come by tomorrow at 3:30?"

The next day, I started the conversation by telling him how much I appreciated his time and what I hoped to accomplish. We proceeded to talk at length about opportunities in the industry. Afterward, he gave me a few hypo-

continued

thetical trading scenarios and asked about my strategy for each. Then he launched into a description of the firm's training program and its advantages over the rest of the industry. He closed by saying, "We don't have any openings right now. But if you're interested, call me in two months. We should have something then."

In the interim, I continued to do informational interviews and industry research. When I called back, they had an opening and I took it.

So few people are resourceful enough to make a phone call like this that you will probably get a favorable response. After all, people who list themselves as alumni contacts wouldn't do so if they didn't genuinely want to help. Even if the person isn't helpful, so what? You haven't lost anything more than a phone call.

Another way to find potential contacts is to read the magazines and newspapers that cater to the industry. Local editions are especially helpful because they often include interviews with local executives. These are the people you want to call. I know this works because I've done it myself on several occasions. Most people are so thrilled anyone saw their name in print that they are more than willing to help. When it comes to business publications, it even works to contact the person who wrote the article, because the writer often specializes in the industry. As such, he or she can be a valuable resource.

One writer I contacted spent forty-five minutes on the phone sharing her insights. When we finished, she proceeded to give me her home phone number along with the best times to call. To this day she wouldn't know

me if I dropped dead in front of her. But she was no less willing to help.

Preparing for an informational interview

Getting someone to agree to an informational interview is only the first step. Next, you have to create a targeted, thoughtful list of questions to ask. Remember, since you asked for the interview, you are in charge. You will be the person asking the questions. The other person may use the interview as an opportunity to ask you questions as well, but don't expect it.

Above all, remember that anyone who grants an informational interview does so with the expectation that he or she will not be put on the spot for a job. Don't violate this trust. Although you won't be asking for a job, you will still be evaluated. Treat it as a formal interview and act accordingly. As the person who requested the meeting, it is your responsibility to guide the conversation. You should have at least two primary objectives: (1) to learn as much as possible about a company or industry, and (2) to explore the many ways to market yourself more effectively.

Depending on the person's position or title, you may have to use a variety of different approaches. This shouldn't matter, but it often does because high level executives, like CEOs, tend to be extremely protective of their time. These executives, if they even grant an informational interview, often do so only as a favor to someone else. For this reason, many have an almost scripted speech prepared for just such an occasion.

Chief executives

If you're fortunate enough to line up an interview with a CEO or top-ranking officer of a company, congratulations—you have earned a wonderful opportunity. But be prepared, since these can be the toughest people to impress. Unlike people in middle and lower management, CEOs are often bombarded by friends and acquaintances acting on behalf of their children, and their time is extremely valuable.

In general, CEOs have a different recruiting perspective. A CEO isn't motivated by the financial incentives or corporate recognition that mid-level managers often receive for recruiting top candidates, so you'll need a slightly different strategy.

CEOs are the only executives I have encountered who will grant an informational interview not to answer questions, but to deliver a canned lecture on the "very specific needs" of their company. With this agenda in mind, not one executive ever

stopped to find out whether I had any relevant experience, because they assumed I didn't.

My first meeting with a person in upper management took place during my senior year in college. After listening patiently to the COO (chief operating officer) describe his company and the fact that they never hire people right out of college, I knew I needed a new strategy—fast. Inspired, I said: "Well, perhaps you can help me in a different way. I have an interview tomorrow morning with an executive vice president at Foote, Cone & Belding. Could you take a quick look at my résumé and tell me what I might do to improve the way I'm marketing myself?"

Realizing he was no longer on the spot to give me a job, he relaxed completely and looked over my résumé. Fortunately, the résumé communicated my accomplishments and qualifications in a way that captured his interest. Suddenly, I was exactly where I wanted to be—selling myself in a two-way conversation. He even gave me a few helpful tips. Not two hours later, a senior vice president from the same company called me at home. The COO had given him my name. The company that "didn't hire people right out of college" suddenly wanted me to come in for an interview!

In order to get the maximum benefit from your informational interview, you must interview the interviewer. This is a four-step process:

1. Ask questions that encourage interviewers to reveal how they evaluate candidates.

2. Rephrase the answers as a questions.

3. Answer the questions as if you were in an interview.

4. Ask for feedback.

Here's how the dialogue might occur:

Candidate: "In this industry, what do people in your position look for in an entry-level applicant?" (Note: This question is more objective and less personal than "What do you look for . . . ?")

Interviewer: "Three things: X, Y, and Z."

Candidate: "So, you want to know X, Y, and Z? To convince an interviewer that I have potential in those areas, I would probably discuss experiences A, B, and C. Experience A demonstrates X because . . . B demonstrates Y because . . . and C demonstrates Z because . . . (pause) Is this an effective approach? How might I be more convincing?"

In effect, this line of questioning leads the person through his or her own interview—answers first. Because this is an informational interview, you can practice your own answers in a trial and error format. This provides access to instant feedback, constructive criticism, and coaching. Depending on how helpful the other person is, you may reach the end of the interview and find that he or she is sold on your potential.

Human resources

With certain exceptions, I have found interviews with human resources people to be fruitless. Not once have I ever made it past the initial screening. In contrast, I have been invited back for additional interviews almost every time I talked with someone from a specific department. Strangely enough, I've talked with a number of executives who had the same experience.

Whenever possible, talk to the people with whom you will be working. This makes sense because you need to evaluate them as much as they need to evaluate you. Furthermore, you cannot possibly get all of your questions answered by someone who has never worked in the field.

For career changers, it's especially important to avoid human resources because often the people in charge of recruiting have an extremely narrow scope through which they search for potential candidates. As a result, it's far easier, and less risky, to present candidates who already have experience in the field. Relatively few human resource professionals I have encountered have the insight to recognize or the conviction to endorse talented people who lack industry-specific experience. Most don't want to take the chance.

When I was working as a headhunter, I found a candidate named Christy who I knew would be perfect for one of our clients. Although Christy had worked in a different industry, she had a dynamite track record. When I presented her paperwork to our human resource counterparts at the client, they immediately rejected her. Not willing to give up that easily, I urged them to let me show Christy's paperwork to a hiring manager. That way, the human resource people wouldn't be the ones to risk looking stupid if the hiring managers didn't agree with me. Fortunately, our client agreed and I presented the candidate to a manager who hired Christy two weeks later.

Unfortunately, not all career changers are that lucky. For this reason, they have to work even harder to convince potential employers to take the risk.

> Ideal conversation must be an exchange of thought, and not, as many of those who worry most about their shortcomings believe, an eloquent exhibition of wit or oratory.
>
> —*Emily Post*
>
> Men should be what they seem.
>
> —*Shakespeare*

The follow-up

The only difference between informational and formal interviews is in the follow-up. At the end of an informational interview, ask the person to suggest names of people you might contact at other companies. Then set the expectations for a continuing dialogue by asking permission to follow up later to see if the person has heard any interesting leads.

You won't be perceived as a desperate pest if the person honors your request and expects your call. For many people, feeling like a pest is one of the major fears that keeps them from following up the way they should. That's why it's so important to manage expectations ahead of time by asking permission to follow up. Once you have permission, ask when the person would like you to call. If he or she says, "Call me next week," then call next week. Don't wait until the week after next or you might give the impression that you either aren't reliable or aren't really interested. Either way, you lose.

If you can't reach the person, leave a message and wait a few days or a week before you call again. While there is no set opinion on what separates a persistent person from a pest, I generally don't leave more than one message a week unless there's an urgent reason to get in touch sooner.

Keeping in touch is also a good way to remain "top of mind" with your contacts. These people may be too busy to call you when they hear about opportunities. It might not even occur to them. However, if you're persistent, there's a good chance that people will remember you at the right time for the right reason.

What Is an Interview?

An interview is a two-way conversation intended to help the candidate and the employer assess mutual fit. As self-explanatory as this might seem, it is precisely the two-way nature of this communication that people forget. This is particularly true of recent college graduates who feel anxious about the job search and self-conscious about their lack of experience.

Entry-level candidates shouldn't spend any time or energy apologizing for their lack of experience—especially in an interview. The assumption that potential employers will react negatively to the absence of full-time experience is both false and dangerous. Any company that takes time to interview college graduates is fully aware that their practical experience will be limited or non-existent. If you had industry experience, you wouldn't be interviewing for an entry-level position.

The same is true for career changers. Focus on your potential rather than your lack of industry-specific experience. It's much more impressive to hear fearless enthusiasm than self-conscious apologies.

For the most part, the specific needs of a company will dictate the way it assesses potential. Listed below are eight broad categories that can apply to any profession. Use this list as a starting point as you match your skills with the needs of a particular company.

Interpersonal skills

When companies assess interpersonal skills, they look for a broad range of qualities that impact how well you interact with others. This often requires a balance of seemingly opposite traits. For example, are you assertive yet flexible? Competitive yet coop-erative? Direct yet tactful? Independent yet a good team player?

If you are being groomed for a management position, you would do well to have examples that demonstrate your ability to coach, mediate, and inspire the people on your team. The most effective leaders also work collaboratively, encouraging the participation and input of everyone on the team.

As a leader or manager, your ability to be proactive and your willingness to take risks will be important. Other valuable qualities include patience, empathy, persuasiveness, and self-confidence.

Analytical ability

Most people think about analytical ability as an ability and comfort level with numbers and calculations. That's definitely part of it. However, if you're someone who struggles with math, don't panic. In a broader sense, your ability to recognize issues and identify potential solutions also falls in the category of analytical ability.

Problem-solving skills

Closely related to analytical skills, this measures your ability to recognize opportunities to improve processes, relationships, and any other issues that arise. Many people spend their personal and professional lives complaining about problems. Relatively few take the time to analyze the underlying issues, formulate potential solutions, and solve the problems.

To assess this ability, interviewers often ask questions like, "If you could change one thing about your college education (current job, etc.), what would it be and how would you go about doing it?" People who are proactive, analytical problem solvers not only recognize opportunities for improvement, but also have taken steps to address them. If this describes you, don't be afraid to mention it in an interview. So few people are proactive that it can be a powerful selling tool.

Writing ability

Depending on the position, your ability to communicate effectively in writing may be one of the most important skills you can offer a potential employer. The content of anything you write will be evaluated on its conciseness, the quality of the content, and whether it is grammatically correct.

Don't underestimate the importance of this ability. Even in the business world, relatively few people seem capable of constructing a convincing, error-free letter. Unfortunately, a college degree doesn't guarantee any level of proficiency when it comes to written communication.

Personality

In addition to the interpersonal skills, interviewers will evaluate your overall personal-ity. In general, they want to see that you are confident, engaging, mature, motivated, and optimistic. To make sure these qualities shine through, relax, smile, and be yourself. If you're too nervous, it may be hard to convince anyone that you are motivated, confident, or engaging.

Another important quality is integrity. For most people, integrity—or lack of it—comes across nonverbally in the way they present themselves. However, it isn't unusual for a company to ask questions or present scenarios to measure integrity more directly. In either case, it's nothing to worry about. You either have integrity or you don't.

Communication skills

Effective oral communication is measured not just by how concisely and directly you speak, but by how well you listen. When people ask you questions, are you able to get right to the point or do you ramble and qualify your answers with unnecessary detail?

If speaking clearly is an issue, consider finding a voice coach. For example, some people who speak English as a second language have such a heavy accent that they are sometimes difficult to understand. Through voice coaching, I have seen people improve so dramatically that they spoke more clearly and used better grammar than most people born in the United States.

Although you might not think it would be an issue, poor grammar is a major obstacle for many people because it makes them appear less intelligent and less capable. That may not be the reality, but it is definitely the perception. For example, I know many otherwise intelligent people who routinely start sentences with "Him and I" or "Her and I" when they should be saying "He and I" or "She and I." It may be nothing more than a bad habit, but it still impacts how people perceive them. If this describes you, challenge yourself to change the habit. It will have profound, positive implications on the impressions you give others.

Idea generation

Idea generation goes beyond problem solving because it incorporates the ideas and improvements that aren't necessarily created in response to an issue.

I remember one candidate, Jennifer, who came up with an idea that literally saved her company millions of dollars annually in shipping costs. Even though she was an intern, Jennifer convinced the company's management that her idea had merit. They agreed and implemented her plan. Based on this alone, I gave Jennifer high marks and recommended we hire her. From a personality standpoint, I knew she was not as polished as most of the people we hired, but it didn't matter. Unfortunately, Jennifer decided to be "humble" and left this important fact off her résumé. To make matters worse, she didn't mention it to any other interviewer. As a result, I was the only person who recommended hiring her.

Not long after the interview, the people in charge of human resources called me into their offices to discuss this candidate. Specifically, they were surprised I recommended someone who had received fairly low marks from everyone else. When I told them the story, the woman in charge of recruiting looked at me and said, "Good for you for finding that out. And shame on Jennifer for not telling anyone else."

Don't be humble. If you've had an idea that made a difference in work or in life, share it.

Adaptability

Adaptability is a big issue for every company because no two corporate cultures are alike. As a result, companies do their best to identify candidates who seem capable of making a seamless transition to the company. In this sense, flexibility and adaptability are essential.

People most likely to succeed demonstrate adaptability through resourcefulness, resilience, and an ability to manage stress. At the same time, they are willing to cooperate and compromise. All of these qualities not only help people adapt to change, but also make them more attractive to potential employers.

The challenge, for applicant and interviewer alike, is to cover these eight categories in a forty-five-minute interview. To accomplish this and still leave time for the candidate's questions is even more difficult. If you didn't realize the evaluation covered so many areas and you weren't fully prepared, getting hired would take a miracle. As it happens, this is precisely how companies rely on applicants to eliminate themselves. The selection process is rigorous, but for better or worse, the applicants always make it easier.

> Nothing so much prevents our being natural as the desire to seem so.
> —*Duc de la Rochefoucauld*

> It ain't braggin' if you kin do it.
> —*Dizzy Dean*

An Interviewer's Philosophy

On a practical level, one of the few differences between a job offer and a marriage proposal is the purpose of the relationship. Whether the agreement is to create babies, ideas, or widgets, the relationship requires time, effort, commitment, communication, patience, and understanding. It hardly makes sense that two people could comfortably enter into a serious relationship after spending a full day or less together. Yet, it happens in the job market every day. I never thought much about the nature of the recruiting process until I became an interviewer myself. Only then did I ask the questions that eventually defined my philosophy:

How might interviewing be different if we entered jobs the way we enter marriages?

As a job hunter, you are about to make a commitment to spend more waking time with a person than you would with a spouse. Isn't that a sobering thought? When you think about it in these terms, it makes sense that interviewers and interviewees alike would do well to approach these meetings differently than we have in the past. Too many interviewees view interviews as one-way interrogation sessions. Too many interviewers don't take the time to think about the skills, experiences, and personality traits that determine whether the candidate is a good fit for their company.

If I had only forty-five minutes to meet and interact with a woman before we decided whether to get married, what could each of us do to make a more informed decision? What would I want to know about her? What would she want to know about me?

For starters, I wouldn't waste a lot of time asking questions like, "Where do you see yourself in ten years?" What difference does it make if your spouse pictures you together at parent-teacher conferences? That won't tell you anything about the success of your marriage or the evolution of your relationship.

Instead, it makes more sense to delve deeper into values, hopes, and dreams. That's what really matters as you develop as individuals and as a couple. Not coincidentally, it's also part of what dictates the long-term satisfaction that comes in professional relationships.

Do I know myself well enough to provide an accurate picture of my goals, strengths, weaknesses, interests, idiosyncrasies, and preferences? Do I listen well enough to appreciate and take the thoughts and opinions of others into consideration?

These questions are as important for interviewers as they are for couples. To successfully identify the best coworkers, interviewers should be painfully honest about whatever it is that they bring to the table. No one likes surprises—especially of the unpleasant variety. That's why it's important for interviewers to be honest about the relative merits of the position, the company, and their ability as managers. Of course, this level of awareness is useless if the interviewer doesn't share it or if the candidate fails to ask.

My approach

As an interviewer, my goal is to minimize the risks associated with entering into a professional relationship. The following questions guide my evaluation:

- Can this person excel in the position?
- Will he or she add value to the team?
- How does this person think?

- How might this person behave in stressful or difficult situations?
- Does this person have the confidence and maturity to express a different point of view without being disagreeable?

My goal is to evaluate the candidate's potential in the context of a relaxed yet challenging conversation. Since the interview is a two-way exchange, I also provide honest answers to any and all questions, and I expect the same in return.

After meeting and shaking hands, there may be a few minutes of casual conversation that can be initiated by either person. For example, the applicant might express an interest in a picture on my office wall. Likewise, I might want to know more about a personal interest listed on the individual's résumé. Whatever the case, this pleasant, brief exchange allows us to absorb our surroundings and establish common ground. It is also important because it can begin to reveal the person's level of enthusiasm and passion for life.

To create a relative level of comfort and to ensure that the candidate focuses on my questions, I say,

With luck, I will be asking questions you have never been asked. At times it might seem like you will never get to tell me about your interesting, career-related experiences. Don't worry. We will have time toward the end for you to tell me anything and everything you think I should know. At that point you can ask me any questions at all. If you ask it, I'll answer it. That includes questions about the interview itself and why I ask what I ask.

This technique minimizes the chance that the person will become preoccupied and nervous when he or she realizes that I haven't asked specific questions about his or her internship, college courses, or experiences abroad.

For the most part, I don't ask questions in any particular order. Some issues need to be probed in greater detail, so I improvise. Like any good conversation, an interview requires flexibility and "give and take" by each party. For this reason, I strive to guide rather than control. People who do well in my interviews have at least four characteristics in common:

❓ The best candidates have conducted a thorough personal assessment.

Without a doubt, this is where most candidates fall apart. Oftentimes, students and other newcomers to the job market just haven't taken the time to think about who they are, what they have to contribute, and why they'd excel in a particular career path.

❓ The best candidates are honest about their strengths and weaknesses.

People would probably be more honest about their strengths and weaknesses if they had taken the time to think about what they are.

> To be able to practice five things everywhere under heaven constitutes perfect virtue . . . gravity, generosity of soul, sincerity, earnestness, and kindness. —*Confucius*
>
> If men could regard the events of their own lives with more open minds they would frequently discover that they did not really desire the things they failed to obtain.
> —*André Maurois*

It amazes me how many people hear questions like, "What did your last boss most appreciate about you as an employee?" and respond, "Well, I was always on time." That may be true, but there are plenty of people who show up on time and fail to accomplish anything.

❓ The best candidates understand the qualities that are essential for the position.

Using the techniques described in previous chapters, it doesn't take much effort to discover the qualities that companies in any industry seek in potential employees. However, this is an effort very few people ever make. That's unfortunate because it's almost impossible to convince people that you are the person they're looking for when you don't even know what they want.

The Importance of Choosing Your Boss

All job hunters—regardless of age, education, or experience—are solely responsible for their own happiness. Some people are so desperate to find a job and so anxious to please potential employers that they don't ask hard questions. However, these same questions can earn the respect of people who prefer employees with a backbone.

Laura had been out of school less than two years when she considered her first career change. At first she was confused by her own sense of urgency. After some reflection, Laura discovered that it wasn't because she disliked her job. Like many young people, she just didn't feel she was where she needed to be. She wanted to move on. Gradually, she realized that her current job put her in an enviable position because it gave her the luxury of waiting for the right opportunity.

In the course of her new job search, Laura was invited to meet with an executive who was expanding his department. Before her appointment, she conducted a series of informational interviews to learn more about the company. Although the job seemed interesting, she was surprised to hear people refer to a widespread morale problem. What disturbed her more was the fact that people in different departments all blamed the same person—the executive Laura was scheduled to meet.

Laura rationalized her reluctance to discuss the issue during her initial meeting by saying, "I don't want to make waves. I know myself well enough to know I can work with almost anybody. This isn't an issue." As the interview approached, however, she was in conflict. Part of her continued to say, "Don't worry. This is a great opportunity." Another part felt tense and uncertain, delivering the opposite message.

In an effort to understand her inner turmoil, Laura turned to meditation. She cleared her mind and began to listen to her body. After a few minutes, a picture formed in her mind. She could see herself standing on the edge of a cliff overlooking an abyss. She associated the edge of the cliff with the hopelessness she felt before getting her first job offer and could feel her body shift slightly, but somehow "hopelessness" didn't quite fit.

Afterward, Laura did not see herself as a potential victim of forces beyond her control. Instead, she felt both trapped and responsible. This led to a profound shift in her awareness and understanding. Specifically, she knew that if she were wrong about her ability to work effectively with the executive people had been complaining about, she could only blame herself. From this came two crucial insights: (1) If the prospect of discussing employee morale seemed difficult now, it would only get harder when she became the person's subordinate. (2) She could mention the issue as an observation—without assessing blame—and ask the executive what plans, if any, were in place to address it.

Despite Laura's best efforts at diplomacy, the executive became agitated at the mention of employee morale. When he denied that a problem existed, Laura had to face the truth. The most interesting job in the world couldn't offset the unnecessary stress of having this person for a boss.

Shortly after the interview, Laura decided to withdraw from consideration. However, not wanting to miss an opportunity for growth, she called the executive to hear his impressions. He shared the following contradictory observations: She was "overly confident" for a person with "such limited experience," and she wasn't the right person for the job because he feared she was someone who would "get bored too quickly."

The first statement, by itself, might have been a valid observation. But it doesn't make sense given his second statement. A person at risk of becoming "bored too quickly" is more likely to be overqualified than underqualified.

At this point Laura could have called the friend who arranged the interview, thanked him for his efforts, and focused on other opportunities. Somehow, that didn't seem like the right approach to her. He wasn't just a friend; he was president of the company. Had their roles been reversed and he had been the one who uncovered potential issues, she would definitely want to know—no matter how difficult it was to hear. Besides, this wasn't about her. The job wasn't right for her anyway.

To Laura's credit, she didn't dwell on the negative. Instead, she focused her conversation with the president on what would be possible given effective leadership and enthusiastic employee participation. She was surprised not only by his positive reaction, but also by the satisfaction of knowing she had acted in accordance with her highest values.

Without this discussion, the president would have known only that Laura wasn't interested in the position. As a result, he might not have considered her for future openings. By sharing her concerns, she left nothing to interpretation. As Laura prepared to leave, he tore a page from his notebook and gave her the name of another person to contact. A few weeks later that person became her boss.

> More trouble is caused in this world by indiscreet answers than by indiscreet questions. —*Sydney J. Harris*

> Listen carefully to the voice in your mind as it is getting ready to make a comment, and think to yourself, "Why am I saying this? . . . Is what I am about to say an improvement over maintaining silence?"
> —*Sylvia Boorstein,* **It's Easier than You Think: The Buddhist Way to Happiness**

The best candidates ask insightful questions.

By now it should be apparent that interviewing is a two-way street. You need to interview the company as much as its representatives need to interview you. Nevertheless, countless candidates leave interviews without asking a single question. It doesn't matter if you've already had 100 interviews at the company, ask questions. Even if you ask the same question you asked everyone else, ask it anyway. Otherwise, you risk looking disinterested.

People who struggle in my interviews haven't thought enough about who they are and what they hope to accomplish. I don't expect people to be fortune-tellers, but I do expect to hear compelling testimony about the choices they've made and the lessons they've learned.

I never ask nebulous, meaningless questions like, "Where do you see yourself in five years? Ten years? Fifteen years?" An insightful, motivated person will evaluate circumstances and opportunities as they develop. There is absolutely no way to know where any of us will be in five years. Nor is it important. There are better ways to assess interest, motivation, and commitment than by asking essentially factual questions about career paths.

Other Interviewing Styles

As you may have already discovered, there are as many interviewing styles as there are people. Some of the interviewers you will encounter have received formal training, while others haven't. Though it's not possible to prepare you for every eventuality, this next section will cover a wide range of styles and questions. Just knowing what to expect can do a lot to alleviate anxiety. While some interviewing styles are more challenging than others, if you take the time to do the self-analysis suggested in this book, you'll be well-prepared to handle any situation. You may even enjoy yourself.

Generally speaking, every interviewer should strive to answer the same two questions:

- Can this person excel at our company?
- Do I want this person on my team?

> No one can make you feel inferior without your consent.
>
> —*Eleanor Roosevelt*

While there are as many different approaches as there are interviewers, your preparation for each will be the same. You must know yourself. This includes an arsenal of concrete examples that demonstrate your strengths, commitment, and abilities.

As an applicant, your top priority is to manage the impression you create. Regardless of the interviewer's style, you need to communicate the same core skills to every interviewer. Having completed a thorough self-analysis, you now have a variety of personal examples to demonstrate the qualities that are important to potential employers. Think of this as a mental checklist of qualities you want to highlight in every interview.

High-stress interviews

For whatever reason, some interviewers do nothing to make candidates feel comfortable. Instead, they do everything imaginable to make them squirm. Although it's less common, it is a style you should be prepared to handle.

High-stress interviews take many forms. Some interviewers ask rapid-fire questions, while others challenge every answer. Whatever the tactic, it's nothing more than a game and you should approach it that way. Think of it as an ongoing battle between you and an opponent whose sole objective is to search for inconsistencies in your answers. Above all, don't let the interviewer put words in your mouth. If you hesitate or change your mind, you've lost the battle.

Most interviews, stressful or not, are structured around a series of questions that each recruiter uses to assess candidates. However, some insightful recruiters use untraditional methods to achieve the same objectives. One executive I know doesn't ask any questions at all. Instead, he gives a brief introduction and allows the candidate to run the meeting. This typically includes an impromptu presentation by the candidate as well as questions for the interviewer. Not coincidentally, this is the same challenge that executives in his firm face every day. Is this approach demanding? Absolutely. Is it unfair? Definitely not. Is it stressful? That depends on the person.

Stress, if it exists, is a function of the candidate's expectations and interpretations. To see how this works, imagine how different people might respond to the interviewer described above.

Candidate 1

Expectation: *The interviewer will ask questions, evaluate my answers, and make a hiring decision.*

Response/Interpretation: *"Wow! I can't believe he isn't going to ask me any questions. He's really putting me on the spot. This is pressure."*

Candidate 2

Expectation: *The interviewer's primary objective is to evaluate my potential given the needs of the company. His method will be a matter of personal preference.*

Response/Interpretation: *"What a great opportunity! I've done my homework. I know what qualities are important to this company. And I know how I've demonstrated potential in those areas. This will be easier than I thought."*

> In skating over thin ice, our safety is in our speed.　　　—*Emerson*
>
> Facts do not cease to exist because they are ignored.　　　—*Aldous Huxley*
>
> It's one of the great biological wonders of the world that there are more horses asses than there are horses.　　　—*Joseph S. Sullivan (attributed)*

In each case, the executive's behavior was the same. Only the expectations and interpretations differed. This example reveals that stress is an internal phenomenon rather than an external one.

Handling Inappropriate Questions

Questions about religion, ethnicity, marital status, or family planning are illegal in any recruiting circumstance. The fact that many interviews are not conducted by professional recruiters is never an excuse for illegal, inappropriate, or sexist comments or questions. Unfortunately, because these questions do arise from time to time, you'll need to be ready. How you respond may depend on two factors:

■ **Whether the interviewer's approach is out of character for the company.** Is this an isolated event or have you noticed other examples of poor judgment and unprofessional conduct?

■ **How badly you want the job.** Are you willing to remove yourself from consideration solely on principle? Is it possible to diplomatically avoid the question with your integrity intact?

In handling inappropriate questions, there are three tactics you might consider. Whichever you choose, be professional and move on quickly.

1. **Gently remind the interviewer that the question is both inappropriate and irrelevant.** You may be absolutely correct and a pillar of diplomacy, but that won't change the fact that you may involuntarily remove yourself from consideration. Of course, that may be for the best.

2. **Rephrase the question in a nonoffensive way before responding.** Perhaps you are a woman who has just been asked, "Do

you think you will want children in the next three to five years?" Using this approach, you might respond, "It sounds as if you have concerns about my commitment to my career. I am extremely committed—I assure you. Whether or not I decide to have children will in no way impact my dedication or performance."

3. **If you recognize the question as inappropriate but you don't strongly object, answer the question if you feel so inclined.**

Next steps

After the interview—preferably the same day—inform the company's human resources department of any questionable encounters. These are the people responsible for educating interviewers and discouraging unprofessional behavior. If you're uncomfortable doing this in person, you might consider putting your thoughts down in a letter. Either way, do your best to remain as objective and even-tempered as possible, regardless of how offended or upset you are.

Before you initiate any potentially difficult or uncomfortable conversation, it's helpful to be clear about your objective. For example, it might help to approach the issue as an opportunity to save future candidates from the same situation. Thinking of yourself as a representative for future candidates may also help you take the situation less personally. On the other hand, if you approach the issue from the point of view of an offended candidate demanding

an apology, you may be 100 percent justified, but you'll also risk coming across as someone who takes him- or herself too seriously.

Completing Your Mental Checklist

As an interview progresses, refer to your mental checklist to make sure you convey the examples that best demonstrate your potential. Near the end of the interview many recruiters ask, "Is there anything else I should know?" At that point go down your mental checklist and mention any qualities and examples you didn't get a chance to discuss. If you have already covered the main ideas, either summarize your qualifications or add a few secondary details. To say "I think we've covered everything" is a mistake because the question is often asked to give you the opportunity to close the deal. Completing the checklist can be difficult in some interviews. If you're running out of time, take charge of the situation:

I noticed that we're almost out of time. Since your job here today is to assess my potential as an employee of this company, I would like to mention a few specifics that are relevant to your evaluation. Does that work for you?

I can't imagine an interviewer who would not be impressed with such a direct and honest approach. Once you get agree-

> Everyone is perfectly willing to learn from unpleasant experience—if only the damage of the first lesson could be repaired. —*Georg Christoph Lichtenberg*

ment, fill in whatever gaps remain and conclude by asking a few direct questions.

If you find it uncomfortable to use this approach, it might help to remember that you're doing both yourself and the interviewer a favor. The fact that you are in this predicament is, in all probability, a result of the interviewer's lack of skill and experience. You may even take some of the pressure off when you refocus the conversation.

Learning from Interviews

To leave an interview thinking, "Great, I nailed it!" or "I can't believe I blew it!" is a waste of time. Unless the interviewer shares his or her impressions, you will probably never know. Never use the interviewer's disposition as a gauge of your performance. Instead, ask yourself the following questions:

- What did the interviewer ask?
- How concisely and completely did I answer each question?
- What, if anything, caught me by surprise?

- How can I better prepare for future interviews?
- What did I learn?

Twenty-two and never been interviewed

My first interview took place on campus during my senior year in college. Although I have repressed the event itself, a productive post-interview evaluation would have focused only on the short list of things I did right. Most of my mistakes could be attributed to a lack of experience, preparation, and confidence.

My most serious mistake was strategic. I should never have scheduled my first interview with the company I wanted most. At the very least, I should have done a mock interview with the career counselors, but at the time that didn't occur to me.

When I finally realized my mistake, I was face-to-face with the recruiter, and my confidence was nowhere to be found. Having done a relatively thorough self-analysis, I knew some of the strengths to emphasize, but I was far from convincing. Worse, I couldn't stop shaking long enough to smile.

My performance was a surprise to everyone—including me. The career counselors didn't think I would need help interviewing because they knew I was as an outgoing, focused, and confident person. My abominable performance was saved only by the recruiter's open-mindedness. I will be forever grateful to that wonderful man for seeing beyond my trembling exterior.

Several weeks after the interview, the company flew me to Chicago for a full day of interviews. Not surprisingly, the recruiter encouraged me to relax and stay calm. I suppose the recruiter knew there was no way I could ever survive seven hours of shaking and sweating.

Unfortunately, I didn't find it necessary to sell myself in each and every interview, and as a result my first choice company didn't find it necessary to hire me. When I heard the news, I told the recruiter (in a nice way) that the company was making a terrible mistake. He replied, "That may be true. Do something else for a year and come back. We never shut the door on anyone."

When I reapplied after graduate school, another recruiter shared some of the written evaluations from the previous year. To my surprise, the individual decisions were exactly opposite of what I would have predicted.

The interview I thought went the worst was with the only person who recommended hiring me. I had written the interview off because I was convinced that the person didn't like me. I'll never forget how uncomfortable I felt when she challenged my answer to the question, "Why advertising?" With a look of frustration, she said, "That sounds like a rehearsed answer—like someone told you to say that."

Shocked, I replied, "I'm sorry you feel that way. It is the truth."

I can see now that my original answer may not have sounded rehearsed. It could have been her way of testing my confidence. Either way, the lesson is the same: be positive and direct, tell the truth, defend your answers, and don't try to guess what the interviewer thinks about you.

During the second full round at my first choice company I sold myself in every interview. Several people even asked, "Why do you think we didn't hire you last year?"

Fortunately, I'd done more than a little thinking about it. As it happened, I had spent too much time trying to make sure everybody liked me and not enough time convincing people I could add value to the company. Having made the first cut, I mistakenly assumed that interviewers would automatically know I had the skills to succeed. That, however, is not the way it works. I should have approached every interview as if it were my only opportunity. In hindsight, the people who interviewed and rejected me reached the only reasonable conclusion. Had I been the interviewer, I wouldn't have hired me either.

Suboptimal interviews

One of the most sensitive situations you can encounter in your job search is an interview where it appears that the interviewer has concerns about you as a candidate. This can be a tricky situation because some interviewers act unconvinced in an effort to see how you will respond. Others are just generally unfriendly and their behavior isn't a reflection on you at all.

If you are absolutely convinced that an interviewer's opinion has turned against you—and it's more than just a challenge of your resolve—you have two choices: continue the interview and do your best to be convincing, or address the issue directly. More often than not you will probably be better off letting the interview run its course. However, if your instincts tell you to take action, approach the issue politely by asking, "Before we go any further, am I correct in thinking you have some concerns I should address?"

For this to work, your delivery must be confident, sincere, and direct. If you sound unsure of yourself, it could raise questions about your leadership and communication skills. If your assessment is accurate, the interviewer will probably be impressed by your direct approach and perceptiveness. You might even sell yourself back into consideration.

When to cancel, reschedule, or cut an interview short

Generally speaking, most people who cancel interviews without rescheduling do so because they have had a change of heart. For example, after setting up an interview with a company in another city, you might realize you're not ready to move. If this happens, just call the company and let them know you've decided not to move at this time, then promise to get in touch if your situation changes.

When location is not an issue and it's the company you don't want to work for, it's still important not to burn your bridges. In this case, when you cancel the interview, keep it general and simple. For example, you

might let them know you need to take a step back to reconsider your options. Since you aren't ready to make a decision, you don't want to waste the company's time. In the interest of diplomacy, it's usually best not to be too specific about your reasons—especially if the observation could be considered judgmental or offensive—because in this era of mergers and acquisitions, the company you reject today might just be signing your paychecks tomorrow. Whatever the reasoning, just make sure you call the company to cancel. There's no quicker way to damage your reputation than by not showing up for an interview.

If you miss an interview because you completely forgot or wrote down the wrong day, it's always best to call and apologize as soon as you realize the mistake. Then follow up with a note of apology. The company may not allow you to reschedule, but at least you'll have the satisfaction of knowing you apologized and accepted responsibility.

Rescheduling, however, is another story. In the event of an illness, family emergency, or any other circumstance serious enough to hinder your performance, call the company immediately and reschedule. While companies generally understand that interviews sometimes need to be rescheduled, it's best to make this a last resort. If you do find yourself in that situation, make sure you have a good reason. An unforeseen medical or dental condition that requires immediate attention would be considered a good reason; missing the home opener for your favorite major league baseball team would not.

If you find yourself running late for an interview, it's always best to call and let the interviewer know. On the day of an interview, borrow a cell phone if you don't have one, because the last place you want to find yourself is trapped on an expressway, stopped in traffic behind some horrendous accident as you watch the dashboard clock tick past your scheduled interview time with no way to call. If the interviewer is unable to accommodate you later than the original time and you have to reschedule, make sure you arrive ten minutes early for the next interview. You are unlikely to be given the benefit of the doubt twice.

For situations that arise after the interview has begun, you'll need a different approach. Although I don't recommend it as a key strategy in your arsenal, there may be times when your best move is to interrupt the interview, cut your losses, and attempt to reschedule.

This happened to me once. As I made my way toward the campus center at Northwestern University for an early morning interview, my head was filled with the usual fantasies: immediate positive feedback, job offers, professional success, and infinite happiness. I don't remember feeling ill, but apparently I was.

After a short wait, the recruiter introduced herself, smiled brightly, and led me to an oversized conference room. The floor-to-ceiling bay windows on the far side of the room revealed a spectacular sunrise over Lake Michigan. As I sat down, the huge windows magnified the already intense rays beating down on my face. I

winced and began to sweat. And sweat. And sweat. I felt worse with each moment, but I kept going.

Fifteen or twenty torturous minutes into the interview, I stood up and struggled to remove my jacket. At that point I should have explained that I felt ill, apologized for the inconvenience, and asked to reschedule. Instead, I ignored a rather obvious problem.

By the time I peeled off my jacket, I was so delirious I couldn't remember what question I was answering. Meanwhile, sweat poured down my face and literally formed a puddle on the floor around me. After forty-five minutes my hair and clothes were soaked. Nothing was even dry enough to wipe the sweat away so I could shake hands and say good-bye. Frosty the Snowman may have melted faster, but not by much.

As I slid outside, I noticed a horrified expression on the next candidate. My appearance left him speechless and traumatized. Realizing what must have been going through his mind, I laughed and said, "Don't worry, she's really nice."

Because I wasn't honest about feeling ill, I performed poorly and eliminated myself from consideration. The recruiter might not have allowed me to reschedule, but I would have been no worse for asking.

Now that you have an understanding of the interview process from the interviewer's point of view, it's time to explore a few of the specific questions you may encounter as you move ahead in your job search.

Analyzing an Interviewer's Questions

If something comes to life in others because of you, then you have made an approach to immortality.

—*Norman Cousins*

To give you a deeper appreciation of the reasons interviewers ask particular questions, this next section will guide you through one of my typical interviews one question at a time. Then, we'll examine a variety of other questions you might encounter. By taking the time to explore the questions as well as what your answers might reveal, you will be better prepared to handle almost any interview situation.

The Big Questions

? **How would you most like to be remembered?**

Your response should include detail and sound reasoning. What is important to you? What are your personal goals? If this seems difficult, approach it from a different angle:

How might you live your life so that if your sixty-year-old self were to meet your twenty-year-old self, they could look each other in the eye, greet each other warmly, and know that they lived admirably and with no regrets?

Because this question deals with personal values, it is not one you should answer in relation to a particular career. It would be a mistake to say that you, as a budding marketing executive, want to be remembered as the person who successfully repositioned Screaming Yellow Zonkers. This not only misses the point, but also risks being a brief and entirely meaningless legacy.

It is also best to avoid any response that leaves the interpretation to the interviewer. For example, it isn't enough to say, "I want to be remembered as a nice person." Nice could imply that you are a thoughtful, kind person who strives to treat humans and animals with respect. Nice is also a totally innocuous word used to describe people—blind dates, for example—who lack exceptional intellectual or physical qualities. If your goal really is to be remembered as "nice," convince me you are living the way you want to be remembered:

- What have you done to realize this goal?
- What have you done that isn't consistent with this objective? Given the chance to relive those moments, what would you do differently?
- What are the biggest obstacles you face? How do you handle them?

What other career opportunities are you exploring?

There is nothing wrong with having other career options. What makes most people interesting is a variety of passions. As a bright, educated person, you have probably

A calm is on the water and part of us would linger by the shore.
For ships are safe in harbor but that's not what ships are for.
—*From the song "Ships" by Michael Lille and Tom Kimmel. Inspired by John Shedd. Downstream Lean Music/BMI*

considered other options. Be honest about the relative merits of each. After all, you have done your homework and have valid reasons for pursuing a particular area of interest. Be persuasive and specific.

To say that the career for which you are interviewing is the only one you have considered will only raise the obvious question: "What will you do if these companies reject you?"

If you could do anything (careerwise) and money wasn't an issue, what would you do?

Even if you never hear this question in an interview, it is one you should ask yourself from time to time. You may be amazed how your answer changes over time. This is a particularly good question to ask yourself at the beginning of your career search and again if you change careers. Never dismiss your talents and interests by saying, "I could never make money doing that." It may help to consult one of the many books that have been written about living your dreams. For example, I highly recommend *Do What You*

> Be not afraid of growing slowly. Be afraid only of standing still.
>
> —*Chinese proverb*

Love and the Money Will Follow, by Marsha Sinetar, because it may open your eyes to what is truly important to you.

Career changers tend to struggle with this issue more than anyone else because even if they strongly dislike their job, they resist the prospect of starting over at a lower salary. Don't let this happen to you. If you truly want to explore a different career, give yourself permission to do so. When I changed careers, I took a 50 percent pay cut, and I don't regret it at all. The truth is, you can adapt to almost any income level. Despite what I expected, my quality of life didn't suffer much either. For the most part, I just curtailed my compact disc addiction. The rest was easy.

❓ If you could take any classes—without regard to credits, majors, or other academic requirements—what would you study?

This question is interesting because of the responses it elicits. Too often, candidates use it as an opportunity to apologize for the fact that they don't have an MBA or other advanced degree. This is the wrong answer. Consider the difference between a positive answer and an apologetic one:

Candidate 1: *What a great opportunity! I have always wanted to take a course in photography. I have some natural talent for composition, but I have never had any formal photographic training. I'd also love to take a few courses in music and art appreciation.*

Candidate 2: *I have thought about getting an MBA. I probably still will at some point. From what I understand, many of my future clients and coworkers already have the degree. It would be nice to speak to them in the same language. If I can't get a job, that's probably what I'll do.*

Each response reveals something different. Candidate 1 views education and learning as an end in itself—a way to better appreciate the world. In contrast, Candidate 2 is preoccupied with the fact that he or she does not have an MBA. To this person, education is strictly a means to an end. Candidate 2 does not appear to have any natural intellectual curiosity—just a warped sense of what he or she thinks the interviewer wants to hear. Clearly, Candidate 1 scores higher for confidence, enthusiasm, maturity, and motivation.

❓ What is one of the best ideas you ever had?

This question is to your career what a "gimme putt" is to golf. It should take almost no thought and very little effort. At some point you should have had a few ideas. Easy, though, the interviewer doesn't want to hear all of them, just one. Your creative solutions to problems and your ability to identify opportunities should be among the strengths you uncovered in your self-assessment. This is your chance to talk about them.

I mentally deduct points for people who look up with surprise and say, "That's a good question. Let me think about it for a second." You shouldn't have to. However, I do remember one impressive exception. The woman sat upright, smiled gleefully and exclaimed, "I've had so many! Let me think about which one was best." I knew instantly that she would be spending a quiet moment weighing the relative merits of a wide range of ideas—not grasping for cosmic enlightenment.

This is probably my favorite question because of the way people react to it. Uninhibited candidates—who are truly passionate about ideas—get a visible adrenaline rush and a wild look in their eyes. Their less enthusiastic counterparts usually have the exact same expression you see when people describe the classic stress nightmare that wakes people up wondering whether they actually graduated from high school.

Unfortunately, most of the memorable responses and ideas were proprietary so I can't reveal them. My favorite non-confidential idea came from a future marketing executive who described her dream of building a house with two dishwashers—so she would never have to unload!

If you could invent anything, what would it be?

This is similar to the previous question, only more specific. The unspoken question is,

"What product or service have you identified that would greatly simplify your life or that of someone else?" Your answer doesn't have to be career related, but the more creative the answer, the better.

At first glance this question might seem marketing-specific. It isn't. What I like about it is that it measures potential in the areas of problem solving, idea generation, and thinking on your feet. In this sense, some level of creative thinking applies to any challenging human pursuit, including architecture, genetic engineering, and electrical engineering.

As you prepare your response, remember that the question doesn't ask for a solution. Rather, it asks you to identify an unmet need. If you have a specific solution in mind, great. But you don't have to.

If I could invent anything, I would invent a tool for peeling pomegranates. Although it's one of my favorite fruits, I rarely eat more than one or two per year. Peeling the leathery skin and separating the seeds from the inner shell is just too time consuming and messy, or maybe I'm too lazy. In any event, it doesn't matter because that's the opportunity I see.

You might be wondering why I used this example to illustrate an unmet need since "need" is a fairly strong word to use in reference to a pomegranate. I just wanted to point out that the question doesn't beg for a "save the world" idea. It's appropriate—even advisable—to have a memorable or off-the-wall response. Necessity may be the mother of invention, but that doesn't mean that laziness, convenience, and fun are never its fathers.

❓ You've just written your autobiography. What is on page 73?

This is strictly a fun question that probes your ability to think creatively and spontaneously. You could also use this opportunity to reveal an interesting fact about yourself that would otherwise never come up in an interview.

❓ What is the most difficult situation you've ever encountered in dealing with people, and how did you address it?

This can be a decisive question. To be successful in any career, you must work well with a wide range of personalities and temperaments. At times you will find yourself in situations that require immediate, corrective action to maintain peace and keep everyone focused on common goals. Not surprisingly, this requires superior listening skills, communication skills, honesty, and leadership.

If necessary, take a quiet moment to structure your answer. Briefly outline the conflict, the alternatives, the solution, and the outcome. Say what you learned, why it was a good experience, and how you might handle it more effectively if you had it to do over.

I will never forget one determined interviewee who described in great detail how he might "collect information" about the person who "didn't like him." It was clear that he would talk to anyone other than the person with whom he had the conflict. I wasn't impressed.

> Flowers grow out of dark moments.
>
> *—Corita Kent*

One of the keys to resolving work-related disagreements is to stay focused on shared professional objectives. I was struck the first time I saw two executives in a heated discussion. When they resolved the dispute, they shook hands. With a quick smile, one said, "It's always business, never personal." Unlike some arguments, I wasn't left with the sense of lingering emotions or unresolved issues. All that remained was a memory of the smile, the handshake, and the profound respect they shared for each other.

No one will ever ask you to love all of your clients, coworkers, or business associates. You don't even have to like them. But if you have to work together, it's critical to maintain trust and respect, stay focused on the objectives, and address problems openly. To get along with people, I've found it helpful to remember my parents' advice: Be genuinely interested in others. You can like anybody if you decide to.

❓ Give me an example of problem solving.

This is as straightforward as it gets. Give me evidence that you recognize and address problems effectively. This doesn't have to be work-related. A roommate conflict, a dispute over an insurance claim, and other personal examples are equally valid. It's a good idea to have as many as ten examples ready. This can include situations that you would handle differently given the opportunity. Discussing an alternative approach also shows that you recognize opportunities for self-improvement.

One interviewer grilled me on this question almost exclusively. By the end of the interview I had been asked for eight examples of my problem-solving ability.

🔲 Give me a personal example of resourcefulness.

Tight deadlines, last minute requests, and unforeseen complications demand a high level of resourcefulness and problem solving from everyone who works as part of a team. Any experience in these areas can be a great predictor of your success on the job.

To uncover examples, start by thinking back to any time when you've been faced with a limited budget. Nothing demands resourcefulness quite like having limited funds. How did you make your budget stretch further? Were you able to trade or barter for services for which you otherwise would have paid cash?

If you need inspiration to be more resourceful, spend time observing a non-profit organization that relies heavily on donated items and funds. Capps Studio, a graphic arts company partially owned by Leo Burnett, used to donate used but usable art supplies to Children's Memorial Medical Center in Chicago. In addition to markers

and paper, the studio collected sheets of foamcore ordinarily used to mount storyboards for presentations. When the people in the Child Life Department at Children's first saw the foamcore, they weren't sure they had a use for it. Before long they couldn't get enough. The patients and staff used it for everything from mounting artwork to creating three-dimensional displays. That's the power of resourcefulness.

Finding your own examples of resourcefulness demands a high level of self-knowledge. Here again, have several examples in mind before you ever send out a cover letter or résumé. This isn't the kind of thinking you'll want to do as the sweat drips down your forehead in an interview.

Questions About Your Personal Interests

If you already have this category on the résumé, the interviewer is likely to inquire about a specific interest. For each, be prepared to give a brief background. But note that it's best to highlight activities you are either currently involved in or were involved in for a long period. It would be difficult to convince anyone you were genuinely interested in anything you did for six months eight years ago.

Also, take the time to describe what motivated you in the first place and keeps you involved. Doing this, you'll convey your passion in a meaningful way. A good answer to the following questions not only demonstrates enthusiasm, sincerity, and commitment, but also convinces the interviewer that you are a relatively interesting person who can interact well with clients, coworkers, and business associates.

❓ Have you ever been recognized for achievement in this area?

When people are genuinely passionate about their interests, it isn't uncommon for others to recognize their efforts. Recognition can take a variety of forms and is not limited to plaques or awards. For example, if your efforts were recognized in a feature article in the organization's newsletter or a local paper, that would be worth mentioning. Even thank-you notes can be worth highlighting—especially when they're from people who were touched by your efforts. Don't be humble. Anything that demonstrates how your participation made a difference is important. Also, get a notebook or album where you can keep awards and letters. If you already have examples of this, don't be afraid to talk about them. Because you worked hard for it, you should feel free to accept the credit you deserve.

❓ What do you cherish most about your involvement?

Whatever the activity, there has to be something about it that captured and continues to hold your interest. What is that? It isn't enough to describe the activity as "fun," since this doesn't explain what encourages you to participate in one activity more than another. Instead, focus on the feelings you get. If you're a skydiver, are you attracted by the excitement, exhilaration, and freedom of freefalling from 15,000 feet? Do you enjoy the adrenaline rush you get doing flips, twists, and aerial acrobatics? Or, is it something completely different?

Questions About Your Influences

❓ Who are your mentors?

Everyone needs at least one mentor. For many, the concept of "mentor" is limited to a specific, formal relationship that exists between a senior- and junior-level person at the same company. This often takes the form of an advisor/advisee relationship where the advisor is an interested third party rather than an immediate supervisor.

But there's more to it than that. The need for a mentor does not stop once you've been at a company for a certain length of time, and it doesn't stop when you become an advisor to someone else. The only thing that stops may be the company's insistence that you have a mentor. This doesn't happen because you no longer need a mentor; rather, it's the company's subtle way of transferring complete responsibility for your development to you—where it belongs. (To learn more about mentors and how you might recruit them, see Chapter 9.)

> Try not. Do. Or do not. There is no try.
> —*Yoda, from* Star Wars: The Empire Strikes Back

? Why are you interested in this career?

This question is often asked of entry-level candidates and career changers who haven't yet worked in a particular industry. In any case, this question demands a two-part approach. First, briefly explain the origin of your interest. By highlighting what you have learned on your own through research and informational interviews, you'll be able to focus on the challenges and opportunities that intrigue you. This will be far more convincing than the vague answers so many candidates fall apart using.

The second and often unspoken part of this question is, "Why would you excel in this career?" Answering this question at the same time will make your response even more convincing. Unfortunately, most candidates don't do this. Nevertheless, this is a great time to demonstrate that you have done your homework. For example, you might say:

> *From talking with people at your company, I understand that you look for people who are critical thinkers, problem solvers, good negotiators, and effective communicators. Given this, I am confident I'd excel here because I*

> *have demonstrated ability in those areas through my experiences at . . .*

To give you an example of an ineffective response, I'll share the classic couch potato answer I heard when I interviewed advertising candidates:

> *Well, I have always loved working with people. I watched a lot of television as a child. For as long as I can remember, I have been more interested in the commercials than in the television programs. I also consider myself very creative. I'm constantly drawing.*

Questions About the Company

? Why do you want to work here?

This question incorporates several unspoken questions that need to be answered to be convincing.

? How much do you know about the company?

Use this opportunity to show that you've done your homework. If you haven't already made the determination that you would work for the company, talk about what you've learned and why you want to learn more. If you already know you'd love to work for the company, support your answer with specifics about the company's performance, employee morale, and other important factors. Then move on to the next unspoken question:

❓ Why would you thrive here?

Even if you haven't made the final determination that the company is a perfect fit, use it as an opportunity to compare your skills and interests with the company's needs. For example, you might ask, "From what I know so far, employees who excel here share the following traits . . . Is that accurate?" If the interviewer doesn't agree with your assessment, find out what traits he or she considers most important. Once you know that, you'll be able to take the answer one step further and describe the traits you share with the company's most successful employees.

If you focus exclusively on the company's reputation without regard to what you have to offer, you may create the impression that you see the job as a springboard to better opportunities. This may be true, but don't say it. The company is much more focused on using you and paying but a stipend for the privilege.

❓ Other than our founder, what famous person—real or fictional—best represents our corporate culture? Why?

Every company, large and small, has its own unique principles that shape employee behavior. What are these principles or philosophies? Are they written as formal operating procedures or simply understood? How would you personify this aspect of the corporate environment? If no single person fits the image, consider a combination.

A strong answer to this question can be supported with quotes and well-known anecdotes. A weak answer is so general it could apply to the figurehead of any company. I like this question because it tests knowledge of the corporate culture in a way that stretches beyond the company's reputation. Just going through the exercise can provide a deeper, more personal appreciation of the companies that interest you.

I was in the midst of my second round of interviews at Leo Burnett when I was asked this question. What has always struck me about the agency is the ongoing, powerful presence of its founder. Although Leo died in the early 1970s, you can almost hear the question "What would Leo think?" echo in the corridors, cubicles, and conference rooms. Even in death, Leo remains the guardian of the agency's ideas. He maintains a quiet watch as his devotees "reach for the stars." After thinking about this for a few moments, the person who seemed most similar in character was Obi-Wan (Old Ben) Kenobi—Luke Skywalker's mentor in the Star Wars trilogy.

Like Leo, Obi-Wan had a quiet influence until he intentionally lost a battle with Darth Vader and the Dark Side. His last words to Vader were, "If you strike me down, I shall become more powerful than you can possibly imagine." Naturally, Vader killed him anyway, and true to his word,

Obi-Wan became the powerful spiritual leader of Luke Skywalker and the remaining Jedi Knights.

Like Obi-Wan, Leo Burnett's presence engages in constant battle with the Dark Side. Before he retired, Leo warned that he too might be forced to return from beyond to do battle with the forces of evil—mediocrity, complacency, and greed. Leo insisted that the company stay true to its mission as long as his name appeared on the door. Otherwise, he threatened to "materialize" and "rub it out" himself (from the speech "When to Take My Name off the Door"). Fortunately, that hasn't been necessary.

The Adjective Questions

About twenty minutes into the interview, I ask the "adjective questions." These are often the most important questions of the interview because of the insights they can provide.

❓ What are five adjectives your best friend might use to describe you?

In this case, my objective is straightforward. I want to know how aware people are of the impressions they make on others. Most people do well on the "best friend" question because they know why people like them. Occasionally, someone will throw in a few adjectives like "detail-oriented" and "punctual." When this happens, I always remind

the person that close, personal friends rarely use phrases like "detail-oriented" when describing each other's most attractive qualities. When you answer this question, be sure you do not include irrelevant personal strengths. Just answer the question that was asked.

❓ Someone who doesn't know you well doesn't like you. What are five adjectives he or she might use to describe you?

This is the most important question of the series. No matter who you are, there will always be people who don't know you or particularly like you. Are you guilty of sending unintentionally negative signals? Be honest, but be sensible. "Mean-spirited" may be a way people describe you, but don't expect the interviewer to reward you for the insight. Believe it or not, I have interviewed several people who described themselves as mean-spirited. When I probed further into their ability to deal with difficult situations, I discovered they were right.

Later in the interview, I'll use your adjectives in a work-related question:

> *You've noticed that a new member of your team has become standoffish. It occurs to you that this person perceives you as "arrogant, driven, withdrawn, critical, and condescending." How would you handle the situation?*

This question is meant to assess how objective, honest, and proactive you are. The ability to build good working relationships with people who may not like you is critical in business, and interpersonal skills can be your greatest strength or your biggest obstacle.

❓ What are five adjectives I might use to describe you?

As someone who doesn't know you well, the interviewer who asks this question wants to know how you think he or she perceives you. Overly self-conscious candidates rarely have a clue. They are too busy worrying about how uncomfortable they are. While it's normal to be nervous, be sure to also stay alert to the impressions you create.

On more than one occasion I've heard candidates say, "I have absolutely no idea how you'd describe me." This always gets my attention because people who truly don't know how others perceive them wouldn't know how to adjust their approach with different personalities. Considering the different personalities you would encounter in even the smallest firm, this is clearly not a selling point. Quite the contrary. It will encourage me, as the interviewer, to probe even more deeply on interpersonal skills. If my initial concern holds true, you won't get the job.

❓ You've known me now for about twenty-five minutes. What are five adjectives you might use to describe me?

Your response to this question provides a glimpse of your ability to interact with and understand unfamiliar people. This is important because, in almost any executive position, you will be asked to present yourself, your ideas, or your products and services to unfamiliar audiences. When this happens, it's important to make fast and relatively accurate judgments about their needs, interests, and perceptions.

Depending on the reaction of the audience, you may also have to shift gears quickly and adopt a different approach. However, if you're oblivious to nonverbal signals, this will be impossible.

While some people are naturally adept at understanding and interpreting the reactions of strangers, there are certain people who are exceptionally difficult to read because they seem to lack emotion. This goes well beyond intentionally keeping a "poker face" to hide their feelings. Unfortunately, there's not much you can do except, perhaps, feel sorry for them for being so out of touch with their emotions.

Beyond the adjectives

Finding appropriate adjectives for any of the questions is only part of the answer. I often probe deeper into the origin of particular traits. For example, when I ask for five adjectives your best friend would use to describe you, I may ask you to elaborate.

Suppose your best friend would describe you as "colorful, fun, trustworthy, driven, and happy." Fun, trustworthy, and happy are self-explanatory. Colorful and driven are not. What makes you this way? If you have already done the thinking, you won't struggle with adjectives or examples to support your statements. Otherwise, you'll waste valuable interview time reflecting on aspects of your personality that should already be familiar to you.

Interviewing the Interviewer

⁇ Do you have any questions for me?

This is the time to remind yourself that you have a responsibility to interview the company. It is imperative that you ask meaningful questions. To help you understand why this is so important, reread the case study entitled "The Importance of Choosing Your Boss" from the previous chapter. Whatever you do, don't ask people how they spend a typical day. It's both expected and trite. Instead, consider some of the following options.

⁇ What do you wish all applicants knew about this company?

This is one of the best ways for you to uncover valuable information because it does not beg for a positive or negative response. It is entirely up to the interviewer's interpretation. If several people at a company respond negatively, morale may be low. On the other hand, you may hear what a wonderful, supportive, family-oriented environment it is. Whatever the case,

you'll be able to make a more informed decision about the company when you receive an offer.

⁇ If you could change anything about this company, what would it be and how would you go about changing it?

This is a good question to ask the interviewer because it may reveal underlying dissatisfaction. Are employees empowered or powerless? If everyone has complaints and no one believes that change is possible, expect to feel the same frustration if you accept the job. Ideally, you will find a healthy environment in which employees are empowered to identify problems and champion solutions.

⁇ Are raises and promotions, in your opinion, based on tenure or performance?"

What you want is the interviewer's opinion rather than the company line. Raises should be based on performance. But, as many companies vigilantly control costs, you might find that tenure is a more important factor. Given the human tendency to use salary as a measure of success, it's important to know what you can realistically expect.

Imagine the following scenario. After one year on the job, you receive an outstanding evaluation and a small pay raise. How do you feel about the possibility that you may not be eligible for another raise for eighteen months? Imagine further that your current boss is a particularly difficult evaluator and you didn't receive high enough marks to warrant a raise. Can you wait another year or two before you get a raise? How would you stay motivated?

Time Management Questions

For the most part, time management questions are straightforward and relate to how you prioritize projects, goals, and other events in your life. The following question, however, is somewhat of an exception, since it asks an entry-level candidate with no work experience to confront a hypothetical situation unlike any he or she has ever faced.

? A client has given you ten projects, but you only have time to do three well. What do you do?

For entry-level candidates who struggle with this question, the biggest pitfall is the common but incorrect assumption that deadlines in the business world are firm and immovable. However, professional life allows a much greater freedom to juggle priorities than we experienced as students. In school, the opportunity to convince a professor to extend a deadline is almost nonexistent. In the business world, flexibility is always available to those who negotiate.

To answer the question operating under the assumption that all ten deadlines are firm sends a powerful negative message. In effect, it indicates a willingness to sacrifice quality for expediency. Unfortunately, this trade-off leads to confusion, resentment, and disappointment. For this reason, this question is about leadership as much as prioritizing and time management.

One of the best approaches to a dilemma like this is to seek the advice of your boss. If the boss is the source of the problem, this conversation becomes even more important because expressing concerns openly is a critical part of teamwork, leadership, and communication.

As you consider the alternatives keep in mind that at most companies work is a team sport. Every decision necessarily impacts the whole team. Thus, effective leaders make sure that everyone understands the dilemma and has an opportunity to offer input. Ideas and solutions can come from anywhere, but they will only emerge when the team feels empowered. Having said that, the interviewer might probe further:

> *Let's imagine you brought the team and client together only to hear the client say that all ten projects share equal priority and must be completed by the same date. What now?*

In a situation like this, the demanding client must assume some responsibility—provided, of course, that your company didn't cause the problem in the first place. At this point you should weigh the relative merits of each project and make a recommendation that outlines expected results by project. If the client doesn't agree with the recommendation, he or she must either state an alternative or communicate specific objections that your team can address. One way or another, everyone must understand and accept the action plan. Uncertainty is not acceptable.

If negotiations fail to yield an acceptable solution, stand firm and promise only what you can realistically achieve. You may have to dig into a reserve supply of courage, honesty, and Zantac—but you'll be glad you did. The value of maintaining your professional integrity and the morale of your coworkers is far greater than the risk of upsetting a client. Unreasonable clients are the toddlers of the professional world. If you make sacrifices to satisfy them this week, how can you possibly tell them no next week?

Creative Problem-Solving Questions

Many of the most memorable and challenging interview questions fall in this category because they call for spontaneous, analytical thinking. For this reason, don't be afraid to take a moment or two to silently consider your answer, and then, in as organized a manner as possible, take the interviewer through your thought process. As you do, you may find that these questions

also offer excellent opportunities to share your personality.

What color is your brain?

This is strictly a fun question that begs for a creative answer. The answer itself doesn't matter. What matters is your confidence. Just be ready to defend your answer. If you say, "I like to think of my brain as a rainbow of bright colors that blend to match my experiences," have specific colors and experiences in mind. It's far better to be enthusiastic and bizarre than self-conscious and uncertain.

Sell me this paper clip.

This is a legitimate question for any career because every business has customers and competitors. To survive, the company must have products and services with meaningful competitive benefits. The question is, what are the benefits?

Whenever you're asked to sell or market a particular product in an interview, approach the problem as if you're the first person ever to see the object. Be enthusiastic about the different uses you discover:

Paper clip uses/benefits

Use 1: *It can hold papers together.*
Benefit 1: *You'll save time being more organized and efficient.*

Use 2: *It can function as a weight on a paper airplane.*

Benefit 2: *By adding weight, the plane will fly farther and you'll have more fun.*

Once you have identified the uses and benefits, you'll be in a better position to describe potential customers, competitors, and the qualities that make whatever product or service you've been given superior.

Without using knowledge from an encyclopedia or any other published source, estimate the size of Mexico in square miles.

If you're pursuing a career that has little exposure to numbers and calculations, don't worry about questions like this because you probably won't hear them. However, if you're pursuing a job that demands a high level of mathematical ability, it is reasonable to expect that your skills may be tested. When I interviewed for a position with an options trading firm, that's exactly what happened. The interviewer told me later that he asked this question to get an idea of how I approached the problem, not to assess how close my answer was to the actual size of Mexico. The interviewer was relatively certain I wouldn't know the exact answer anyway since it qualifies as a very obscure fact. And he was correct; I had absolutely no idea.

To answer the question, I took him through my thought process. First, I estimated that Mexico was roughly as long from north to south as the United States is from east to west—about 3,000 miles. From what I could remember, the country had approximately the same shape as an upside

down right triangle with the base cutting halfway across the United States from California to Texas. I estimated the distance of this base as approximately 1,500 miles. Rather than get into the exact dimensions of a right triangle with sides of x, 2x, and x times the square root of 3, I decided to treat the country like a large box instead of a triangle. That way I could just multiply the length by the width and divide by two to get an approximate answer. As a result, I estimated Mexico to be roughly 2,250,000 square miles (3,000 × 1,500/2)—give or take few hundred thousand square miles.

The interviewer went on to tell me that he liked the way I approached the problem because he hadn't thought about it geometrically. As it happened, he had been asked the same question when he interviewed with the firm and based his answer on a range using some other criteria. To this day I don't know what the square mileage of Mexico is and I have no idea if I was even close. But it doesn't matter because that isn't what the interviewer was looking for anyway. And besides, I got the job.

Continuum Questions

This approach asks that you place yourself on an imaginary range between two specific traits or qualities. Despite its popularity, this line of questioning is artificial, contrived, and shallow. To demonstrate why this is true, let's look at a specific example. Imagine that, as an interviewer, I've just asked a candidate to place herself on a continuum between strategic and tactical. In response, the candidate says, "I definitely fall on the strategic end of the continuum." Would this be the right answer? If "strategic" is what I wanted to hear, her answer was probably correct. But what did I really learn? Even if she pinpoints an exact location on the continuum, so what? I still haven't learned anything. Self-appraisal without example is meaningless. The candidate has done nothing more than describe herself using one of two adjectives I provided.

In some cases, even a theoretical continuum, which I'll get into below, is of limited use. For example, an interviewer might ask you to describe your working style as more strategic or more tactical. In other words, do you prefer to create a plan or execute it? While this question has some validity, strategic and tactical approaches tend to be interdependent rather than mutually exclusive. The ability to get work done is meaningless if your tactics are not based on a sound strategy. Likewise, what good are strategic skills if you lack the tactical ability to champion actionable solutions?

Adjectives on a continuum typically fall into three categories: positive/positive, neutral/positive, and negative/negative. In general, interviewers don't use positive/negative adjectives—for example, nice vs. nasty—because the choice is too obvious.

In some cases, it won't be clear whether the words are positive, negative, or neutral. If you're unsure, think about the words as they relate to the specific needs of the company and make your best guess.

If the decision is between two positive adjectives, the middle ground might seem safest. It isn't. By asking the question, the interviewer wants you to take a stand. Use a four-step approach:

1. Determine which attribute is more important.

2. Acknowledge the importance of each relative to the job requirements.

3. Place yourself to the left or right of center (toward the more important adjective).

4. Give a personal example that demonstrates the more important attribute.

When faced with two negative adjectives and no continuum, you don't necessarily have to answer the question. For example, one interviewer didn't give me a continuum, he simply asked, "Are you the kind of person who works to live or lives to work?" Before responding, I asked for clarification: "Are you allowing for a continuum between the two?" Unsympathetically, he replied, "No. Choose one."

Because I guessed that he was trying to assess my passion, I chose "live to work." In hindsight, picking either extreme was a mistake. I should have said, "Given that we aren't allowing for a continuum, I don't feel comfortable picking either of two dysfunctional extremes." This was the truth. I just didn't have the guts to say it at the time.

Saying what's on your mind and steadfastly defending your own point of view is important for several reasons. First, most employers aren't looking for spineless people who can't form or defend their own opinions. Instead, they want people who have educated opinions and aren't afraid to share them—even when the opinions may be unpopular. It's also important to defend your point of view because many interviewers will challenge you just to see how you respond. It's not unheard of for interviewers to ask questions or make statements that come across as condescending or almost insulting. For example, an interviewer may cut you off mid-sentence and ask incredulously, "You don't really believe that, do you?" If you treat the interview as a game of wits, defend your point of view, and never take it personally, you'll be better able to maintain your composure and confidence. Then you can smile and say, "I sure do, and here's why . . . "

Questions, Questions, and More Questions

Now let's look at some other questions, common and unusual, that interviewers might ask to learn more about you. Some have a single, relatively obvious objective, while others are used to assess multiple attributes like time management, prioritizing, and managing expectations. In order to prepare for them, you should write your answers in your job search journal. The purpose of reveiwing these questions is to be prepared—not rehearsed—so don't use them to memorize standard answers.

Questions about who you are and where you're going

These types of open-ended questions are often challenging because they aren't specific and can be answered in many different ways. People who haven't taken the time to do a thorough self-analysis generally struggle with them. In contrast, those who have given considerable thought to who they are and what they hope to do tend to be much more convincing.

Tell me about yourself

This may be the vaguest and most difficult of all interview questions. If you had a particularly interesting childhood that impacted the person you are today, you might begin with that. In any case, make it clear where you are going. Otherwise, the interviewer will be forced to interrupt your life story when it's clear you aren't using the question to your advantage.

In this case, it's also legitimate to ask for clarification. For example, you might ask the interviewer if he or she is more interested in hearing about you personally or professionally.

If the interviewer gives you a choice or no additional direction, you're better off keeping the focus professional. Start by tracing the origin of your interest in this career. Be sure to share what you learned through research and informational interviews because it will help demonstrate your passion. As you finish, take the interviewer all the way through the present by explaining how you happened to learn about the company and why you're interested in joining his or her team.

❓ Why are you here?

The confrontational nature of this question begs a direct and concise response. In effect, the interviewer is saying that he or she values time and wants to get right to the point. It gives you the opportunity to convince the interviewer that the two of you should be having this conversation.

If you already know you want the company to make you an offer, simply explain how your skills match the company's needs. On the other hand, if your mission is to learn more about the company, you might say, "Overall, there seems to be a good match between my skills and your needs. My goal today is to determine if this is truly a good fit."

The last time anyone asked me this question, it caught me by surprise because the circumstances were so unusual. I'd been working for several months on a freelance project, so I wasn't exactly in interview mode when I met the new senior vice president. Without smiling, he looked me in the eye and in an abrupt but professional way asked, "Why are you here?" After a deep breath, I outlined my experiences and objectives as they related to the needs of the company. Highlighting the company's needs rather than my strengths also helped to take some of the pressure off. But I'd be lying if I didn't admit that it took time to regain my composure.

Direct questions about your potential

Almost every interview question is related in some way to what you can offer a potential employer. When the questions are direct, your answers must be equally direct. In other words, the interview is not the place to be humble or shy about your strengths, abilities, or accomplishments.

❓ You are asked to write a one-page ad for yourself. What is the headline?

Although this question is particularly appropriate for advertising, it could be used in almost any interview. The interviewer wants to know how well you know the product (you) and its benefits (the reasons you would be great at this company). Combine the product and benefit in a short, high-impact headline. It doesn't have to be clever, but it should demonstrate that you understand and meet the needs of the company.

❓ What are your greatest strengths?

This is another opportunity to complete your mental checklist. Use key words and phrases that correspond to the needs of the company, like resourcefulness, problem-solving ability, and strategic thinking. Any time you can sell yourself unabashedly, do it. Be confident, concise, and support your statements with personal examples.

❓ What is one of your greatest accomplishments?

A good interviewer will probe accomplishments the same way he or she assesses problem-solving ability. For this reason, break down each accomplishment into the following categories.

The obstacle/challenge: What would have kept you from achieving your goal? For example, if your greatest accomplishment was being chosen to sing "The Star Spangled Banner" at the Chicago Cubs home opener, what obstacles did you have to overcome? How many people did you compete against for the honor? How many years of voice lessons did you endure to reach that level of ability? Were there any challenges you faced along the way?

To use a different example, let's imagine that your greatest accomplishment was receiving your company's highest customer service award. In addition to the competition from other employees, you undoubtedly faced the challenge of successfully dealing with unhappy or unruly customers.

Possible courses of action: In the first example above, the alternative courses of action would refer to the opportunity cost of years of singing lessons. For example, do you remember missing sleep-overs at a friend's house because you had early morning voice lessons? In other words, what sac-

rifices did you make along the way to achieve what you have achieved today?

In the second example, the possible courses of action varied depending on the circumstances you faced with each customer dilemma.

Specific tactics: For the first example, describe what you did to keep yourself motivated to practice. Were there times when your commitment lagged? If so, how did you handle it?

For the second example, describe what you did and how it differed from the tactics used by other customer service people in your company. Are you a better listener? Are you more resourceful in solving customer complaints? What makes you more effective?

Quantifiable results: In the first example, singing at a major league baseball game is an honor in itself. However, it could become even more meaningful by adding additional perspective. For instance, are you the youngest or oldest person ever to receive the honor? How many people did you compete against?

In the second example, the same questions apply. Are you the youngest or oldest employee to receive the award? How many people were eligible for the award? Is there anything else noteworthy regarding the company's decision to give you the award?

By taking the time to quantify any achievement and then to put it in perspective, accomplishments can become even more impressive. As you describe your accomplishment, a good interviewer will

> We only confess our little faults to persuade people that we have no large ones. —*Duc de la Rochefoucauld*

probe to get a better understanding of your ability and your opportunities to improve further. For example, if the accomplishment you describe relates to superior customer service, the interviewer might ask the following questions:

❓ What specific traits do customers value most in you?

In this case, the interviewer wants to know your level of awareness as it relates to what you already do well. The ability may come naturally to you, but if you can't describe what makes you effective, you may not be able to teach anyone else to get the same results.

❓ I imagine your customers have different levels of satisfaction. What would one of your least satisfied customers say?

Here, the interviewer is basically saying, "Not every one of your customers will ever be 100 percent satisfied 100 percent of the time. If I asked a customer who wasn't always satisfied with your service how you might improve, what would he or she tell me?" In other words, you may be the best, but you still aren't perfect. What steps are you taking to improve?

Direct questions about your shortcomings

Any question that asks you to be brutally honest and critical of yourself can be uncomfortable to answer. What is important is not that you beat yourself up unmercifully, but that you objectively consider opportunities to improve who you are and how you come across.

❓ What are your weaknesses?

Few questions generate as much pre- and post-interview conversation as this. While the concept of self-awareness is valid, the question is so predictable it's become meaningless. Some interviewers will ask this question simply because it's a "classic." A more seasoned interviewer will ask it because he or she hasn't found a better way to assess how well you know yourself.

As discussed previously, the following question comes closer to revealing the truth: "Someone who doesn't know you well doesn't like you. What five adjectives might he or she use to describe you?"

Fortunately, you don't have to know why the question was asked to handle it effectively. Rather than disclosing weaknesses that could damn you to a life of unemployment, answer the following questions:

? Given the qualities that are critical for success, in what area would you most like to improve? What are you doing to make that happen?

Provide evidence that you have worked on the areas you identified. If you haven't already done so, make a commitment to improve yourself both personally and professionally. Otherwise, your first on-the-job evaluation is not going to be an adventure you will be anxious to repeat.

? What one thing would you not want me to know about you?

This is a variation of the ever-popular question, "What is your biggest weakness?" Han-dle it as you would the "weakness" question. For example, you might smile mischievously and start by saying, "Naturally, I'd like to convince you that I am an absolutely perfect candidate with no flaws or opportunities for improvement. But we both know that can't be true."

From there, pick a skill you're committed to improving and focus on that: "So, as much as I'd like you to believe that I am a perfect manager, I know there's room for improvement. That's why I've been taking classes on my own to get better at delegating."

This way, you've answered the question honestly, but at the same time put a positive spin on it to demonstrate that you're committed to improving. What more could a potential employer want?

Following Up and Closing the Deal

The strength of a man's virtue should not be measured by his special exertions, but by his habitual acts.
—*Blaise Pascal*

I n this chapter we'll look at strategies to help you feel more confident as you build and maintain an ongoing dialogue with the people you meet in your job search. One of the most difficult aspects of accepting a job offer is negotiating an acceptable salary and defining your worth, and I'll present tools and techniques to do just that.

Always Follow Up

Most people, because they have an understandable desire not to be thought of as a pest, tend to err in the direction of not following up as they should. That's unfortunate because there are countless people who have earned jobs through sheer persistence.

There are also plenty of people like Laura (see the box in Chapter 6 "The Importance of Choosing Your Boss") who have landed jobs strictly as a result of their follow-up. In Laura's case, after her rejection the easiest course of action would have been to write the original interview off as a learning experience and look elsewhere.

Instead, she took the time to share her perceptions and concerns with the company president because she knew she would appreciate the feedback if she were in his shoes. That one decision literally changed her life because the president, who had arranged the original interview, encouraged Laura to meet with an executive in a different department who hired her.

As you build your network, the best way to avoid being perceived as a pest is by managing expectations upfront. For example, at the end of your informational interviews, ask if it would be all right to call in a few weeks to see if they've heard about any opportunities that might be a good fit. Once you get permission to call, ask when, specifically, would be the best week to do so. Then make sure you follow up in a timely manner. Otherwise you risk being perceived as disinterested and unreliable.

Another strategy to stay in touch with key contacts is to follow up with a brief note detailing your progress. Use each letter as another opportunity to thank people for their time and interest. I remember one woman who followed up with a series of postcards to let me know her current status and to see if I had any suggestions. She used such visually interesting postcards and wrote such funny notes that I always looked forward to the next installment. At the time, I was working with quite a few people who had similar skills, but guess who I thought of first when the right opportunity came along?

While it's important to master the art of following up, it's even more important to remember that the impressions you make begin long before you sit down to write a thank-you note. The impressions also extend to everyone you encounter at the company, not just the person who takes the time to meet with you. It's amazing how many people either forget this or just don't think about it. That's why it's important to be polite and professional whenever you have contact with a company, its employees, and its clients. This includes secretaries, receptionists, janitors, mail carriers—everyone! Leave anyone you meet with a smile.

Making a positive impression is critical for a number of reasons. First, and most important, everyone, regardless of his or her position, deserves to be treated with kindness and dignity. It's also worth remembering that it's not unheard of for hiring managers to ask receptionists and others to share their impressions of a candidate. If you are demanding, rude, or generally unpleasant in the waiting room or anywhere else, there's an excellent chance the hiring managers will hear about it. Rather than take that chance, spend your time and energy practicing kindness and compassion.

Written communication is particularly important, because the way you write reflects not only on you, but also on the company that hires you. For this reason, treat every cover letter, résumé, writing sample, and thank-you note as an example of your professionalism and writing ability. If you struggle as a writer, take a class or read one of the many useful books published on the subject. You don't have to write like a poet or novelist, but you do have to write somewhat proficiently or your chances of being hired are substantially reduced.

Thank-you notes

So few people take the time to write follow-up notes (of any kind) that they convey a powerful, positive message out of proportion to the effort. Thank-you notes are particularly important after an interview. It won't impact the company's decision. Rather, it's common courtesy—which unfortunately isn't all that common—but again, by not following through with this small act, you will substantially reduce your chances of being seriously considered for the job.

Thank-you notes arrive in one of three forms: business letters, notes handwritten on stationery, or greeting cards. When in doubt, the business letter format is the safest option.

If you have multiple interviews on the same day, send a separate note to everyone who interviewed you—and anyone else who went out of the way to make you feel comfortable or introduce you to the company. A single note to the company is not enough. The letters shouldn't be long, and you should include a specific reference to your conversation to help you reconnect with the interviewer. This will be easier if you take notes as soon as you can after each interview, otherwise a full day of interviews will be one big blur. It's also a good idea to get business cards from everyone you meet in order to verify the name, spelling, and title. If for some reason you aren't able to do this, call the company's main number and ask the person who answers for the information.

Phone calls

If you tell somebody you will call on Tuesday, call Tuesday. Otherwise you may be perceived as unreliable. I was fortunate to learn this lesson through someone else's mistake. As I sat in the general manager's office at WUSN-FM in Chicago, a voice came over the intercom: "Steve, Brad on line two is inquiring about the position, will you take the call?" Without blinking, Steve replied, "No. He was supposed to call yesterday. Please tell him we have nothing for him." That was it. Steve wasn't interested in explanations because he already knew that this was a strong indication of how Brad would perform on the job. In this sense, everything you say, do, or fail to do can and will be scrutinized by potential employers. Call when you say you'll call and do what you say you'll do. Always.

Gift giving

Some people are overcome by the urge to buy trinkets and gifts for interviewers. Resist this urge at all costs. Once the interview is over, nothing you can do will positively impact the outcome. A gift will only ensure that you are remembered for the wrong reasons, since it may look like you're attempting to bribe your way into the interviewer's good graces.

The Power of Initiative

Maggie isn't just a dolphin trainer, she's an inspiration. At the same time, she is a wonderful example of what's possible when you choose to overcome obstacles with passion, persistence, and initiative.

What is especially wonderful about Maggie's experience is the wealth of inspiration it provides on so many different levels. Through her perseverance, Maggie not only succeeded in becoming a dolphin trainer at the age of sixteen, but also unknowingly voided many of the convenient excuses that people sometimes use to hold themselves back (e.g., "I'll never get a good job because I don't have a college degree."). After all, Maggie is making her dreams come true and she hasn't even graduated from high school yet.

In preparation for a family trip to Honduras, Maggie, who was thirteen at the time, began taking scuba lessons at a local dive shop. However, like many people, she had problems with her ears that made it painful to be even eight feet underwater in a pool. With just days to go before she and her family were to leave, there was no time to treat the problem with medication. To her great disappointment, it became clear that she wouldn't be doing any scuba diving in Roatan.

Maggie's father immediately started looking for activities on the island to keep Maggie busy while he and her mother were diving. As it happened, the Roatan Institute for Marine Sciences (RIMS), a training and research facility, was connected to Anthony's Key Resort, where they were staying. In conjunction with RIMS, Anthony's Key offered a Dolphin Discovery Camp for children of scuba divers and other vacationers, so Maggie's father signed her up.

On the first day, the children played with the dolphins at the research facility. A few days later Maggie and the group fed sea turtles that were being rehabilitated before being returned to the ocean. Over the next few days, she snorkeled with the dolphins, learned signals used to get the dolphins to perform specific behaviors, and collected shallow water samples to examine under a microscope. By the end of the week Maggie knew she wanted to pursue a career in marine sciences.

The following summer, before she and her family returned to Roatan, Maggie sent an E-mail to the people who ran the camp to let them know she would be back. In her note, she told them she remembered everything and offered to help if they needed it. The camp directors responded to her letter enthusiastically.

During the week, Maggie met Roy, a marine biologist for a university in California. By this time, Maggie had done enough research to know how hard it was to find a volunteer position that would accept someone who was only fourteen. When she shared her dilemma with Roy, he told of his plan to return the following year to do coral research on the reefs of Roatan. Maggie asked if there was any way she could assist, and although he didn't usually accept high school volunteers, Roy suggested that she E-mail a résumé when she got home.

Not wanting to miss the opportunity, Maggie did more than E-mail a résumé. She also sent letters of recommendation. As she puts it: "I basically harassed the man for a while." Sometimes that's what it takes. Maggie's persistence, no doubt, helped convince Roy that she was serious, committed, and would definitely follow through, so he agreed to take her on as his volunteer assistant.

While she was in on the island, Maggie made a point to introduce herself to Teri and Eldon, the couple who ran the RIMS. She told Teri how she got involved with the camp and about her dream to be a trainer there. When Teri found out that Maggie was only fifteen, she was visibly apprehensive. Maggie put together an updated résumé and E-mailed it to her anyway. Not willing to stop there, Maggie asked Roy to put in a good word for her when he returned to Roatan in January. Before long, Teri sent an E-mail with the words Maggie most wanted to read:

> Look forward to seeing you in June. Come as soon as possible and stay as long as you can.

Even though much of the staff seemed apprehensive about her age, it didn't take long for Maggie to prove herself. In addition to learning the art of dolphin training, she learned even more about the hard work that goes along with being a trainer. As Maggie puts it:

> At the time, there were seventeen dolphins at the institute. The dolphins ate three times a day consuming an average of 22 to 25 pounds of fish per dolphin. Multiply that by seventeen dolphins and you've got almost 400

continued

pounds of fish per day to thaw. In addition, each individual fish had to be checked to make sure it was healthy. Afterward, you have to wash everything so it doesn't rot in the heat. That means bleaching everything—the buckets, sinks, the walls, and the floor. So, I've got news for the people who say I have it easy just swimming with the dolphins all day.

But Maggie is quick to add that the hard work paid off. She's sixteen now, she has a job she loves, and she's well on her way to a career in marine studies. And she hasn't even graduated from high school!

One thing I really learned is that marine biology isn't the only field in this area of study. In fact, most trainers are not marine biologists; they are animal behaviorists, animal psychologists, etc. Although I'm not sure exactly what area I will pursue, I know I'll be actively involved in marine studies.

The biggest human temptation is . . . to settle for too little. —*Thomas Merton*

Only when the last tree has died, the last river poisoned, and the last fish been caught, will we realize that we cannot eat money.

—*19th Century Cree Indian Saying*

Not long after one interview, I received a hand-delivered thank-you note and a pair of Nike athletic socks. According to the note, I was supposed to remember the socks when I asked myself whether we should hire this person. Of course, I was instructed to "Just do it!"

Perhaps the use of a famous advertising slogan was supposed to impress me. Who knows? Even beyond the bizarre premise and execution, I was mystified by the ignorance. Why would anyone send Nike socks to a company that represented Reebok? Ouch! Save your creativity and generosity for your job performance once you're hired.

Salary Negotiation

Salary negotiation is a delicate, difficult subject for most people because it is so emotionally charged. To make matters worse, countless people equate their value as individuals with what the market is willing to pay for their skills. This is unfortunate because you don't have to look much beyond teachers and nurses to realize that in our society there is almost no correlation between the importance of the job and the salary employers are willing to pay. Even though salary may be a difficult topic to approach, you must do so because it plays an important role in determining whether an opportunity is right for you.

At the entry level, your opportunity to negotiate is somwhat limited. Nevertheless, you should be prepared to handle the topic confidently—if and when it arises. Compensation is too important an issue to treat lightly. In general terms, think of salary negotiation as a poker game you play with your future income. To win, you must know what to say and when to say it, and above all, don't show your cards to anyone.

Pick the right time

Before responding to a salary inquiry, ask yourself "What stage of the interview process is this?" and "Is the person asking the question a key decision maker?"

If an offer hasn't been extended, it isn't appropriate to discuss salary, because either you or the company may still have questions that need to be addressed first. In this case, a salary discussion will only sidetrack the more important issues. To avoid a premature salary discussion, simply point out that you aren't comfortable discussing salary until

> We know what happens to people who stay in the middle of the road. They get run over. —*Aneurin Bevan*

you're certain that there is a good mutual fit and all issues of compatibility have been addressed.

More than once I've heard from candidates who were grilled on salary questions by low-level employees who have little say in hiring decisions and no input in salary negotiations. If you have a similar experience, your challenge is to shift the focus to more salient issues. For example, you could counter with another question and inquire if the company pays a fair and competitive salary. This response is effective whether or not the person is a decision maker because it puts the pressure on the interviewer—where it belongs. If the interviewer pursues the issue, you have two options. First, if you have outstanding questions (other than salary) that will impact your decision to accept or reject an offer, address them immediately. Inform them that before you discuss salary you would like to take the next several minutes to ask a few more questions about the company and the position.

If you have no further questions, and you know the person is a decision maker, take a deep breath and begin. Otherwise, arrange a meeting with the appropriate person.

The psychology of negotiation

For many people, salary is an emotionally charged issue inextricably tied to their self-image. This is unfortunate because there is no correlation between income, happiness, and your value as a human being. The inability to separate self from salary is also one of the greatest obstacles to effective negotiation.

To replace emotion with objectivity, I often pretend I'm representing someone other than myself. That way, I become less attached to a specific outcome and view it as the fun game it can be. This confident, almost distant approach has two primary benefits. First, it prevents me from making unnecessary concessions. Second, it encourages the other party to work harder toward a deal.

The challenge is to be a tough negotiator without being an obstructionist. On the other extreme, don't confuse desperation with enthusiasm. You are a risk to yourself if your attitude communicates the message that you would take the job at any salary, that you couldn't live without this job, or that your life and happiness are at stake if you don't get it.

If you even get the job—which would be doubtful at that point—this perception will earn you the worst deal imaginable. If you jump at any offer, the company will know you would have accepted less. This can have a substantial negative impact on your perceived value to the company. Some people are so excited by offers and so intimidated by interviews that they abandon common sense when they should be negotiating. "Yes," "Of course," and "That's fine" are not the first words uttered by skilled negotiators. When you begin negotiating, keep two rules in mind: (1) Don't answer questions (or supply information) about your salary history and (2) don't quote specific figures.

Your market value

Believe it or not, your previous salary is irrelevant. The only two factors that should be considered are your market value and your value to the company.

When asked about previous salary, diplomatically acknowledge the person's curiosity while at the same time reminding him or her that your prior compensation is not relevant as it relates to your value to the company. Nor does it impact your ability to excel in the position. By clarifying the company's expectations and your ability to meet them, you can arrive at a fair salary.

The fact is, any company that is actively recruiting should have budgeted for the position. Furthermore, the company's ability or obligation to pay your salary has no connection to compensation agreements between you and a previous employer.

If you're still uncomfortable with the issue, imagine this: a house is for sale at an unspecified price. You like the house but you aren't confident you can put an accurate value on it. Sensing your interest, the owner asks, "How much will the bank loan you?"

If you're smart, you won't respond. Your credit line at the bank has nothing to do with the value of the house. Answering the question makes no sense whatsoever because it gives the seller valuable information while the buyer receives nothing in return. From this point on, negotiation will favor the seller, who now knows the buyer's upper limit. Meanwhile the seller's lowest acceptable price remains a mystery. The buyer hasn't even determined a possible price range. So it goes with salary negotiation.

At the beginning of the negotiation, the company may be reluctant to quote a specific salary. If so, ask about the range. If you know the range, you will have a better chance of negotiating a salary on the higher end.

To quote a specific salary without any information about what the company might pay is a huge risk. If the company has budgeted $28,000 to $35,000 and you state a salary requirement above $35,000 or below $28,000, you can only lose. If the company representatives know they can hire you for $25,000, that's probably what they will pay. It won't matter that the range was higher, because no one is in business to give money away.

If you state a salary requirement higher than the range, you could still lose. If the company's offer is competitive and you quote a salary outside the range, it will be obvious you didn't do your homework. On the other hand, if you know you're worth the premium, defend your position.

How you respond to a company's offer will depend on where it falls relative to the expected range. Acceptable offers, by definition, will either fall within the range or above it. If it falls above the expected range,

your initial response should differ, for reasons I'll discuss later.

When the company makes an offer in line with your expectations, do not accept it right away. Instead, take some time to carefully consider the situation.

Silence is an extremely powerful negotiating tool. While you are thinking, the person on the other side of the desk may spontaneously break the silence by saying, "Of course, we could probably go as high as . . ." If so, congratulations. You have just earned your first raise. Otherwise, smile, let the person know the offer sounds reasonable, and focus the discussion on other specifics like vacation, insurance, profit-sharing, and bonuses. At this point you still haven't accepted the offer, you've just advanced the discussion to get a more detailed picture of the package.

Once you reach an acceptable offer, take at least one night before you commit, but if you need more time, ask for it. Whatever you do, don't be pressured into making a decision too quickly. Over the past few years, I have heard about a number of companies who unreasonably expect people to accept or decline on the spot. If this happens, walk away. There is no legitimate reason for a company to have a policy like this.

Silence can also have a wonderful impact on an already high salary because there may still be room to the upside. Therefore, the same rules as previously discussed apply. However, if a salary falls above the expected range, and in particular if it's significantly higher than the industry standard, it may be a warning flag. In that case, one or more of the following could be true:

The responsibilities of the job differ significantly from your expectations.

It sometimes happens that companies hire people and have higher expectations than the candidate can legitimately meet. A higher than anticipated salary may be a clue to misconceptions and unrealistic expectations. Even company presidents can make this mistake.

For example, Sarah was hired by an Internet start-up company as a vice president of marketing. As it turned out, the president of the company, who did the hiring, assumed she was also a Web designer. The topic never came up in the interview. Instead, the president made the assumption based on the fact that the last marketing person he worked with was a talented Web designer.

Although the misconception wasn't discovered until after Sarah started work, the president accepted responsibility for the error and worked hard to transform it into a win-win situation. Unfortunately, not everyone operates with such a high degree of integrity.

The company has a problem attracting and keeping talent.

At some companies, employee morale is so low and attrition so high that they are willing to pay higher than average salaries. Some people like to think of it as battle pay. This is perfectly acceptable if you know what you're getting into and are willing to take the risk. If not, don't be blinded by the higher salary alone. No amount of money can adequately compensate for an abysmal work environment.

The cost of living is higher in that particular city.

Although there are salary calculators available on the Internet that estimate the cost of living in particular cities, I haven't seen one that is accurate enough to recommend. Instead, you would be better off talking with people in similar positions to determine what is realistic. In places like New York, the cost of living is so high—compared to Chicago, for instance, and other major cities—that an extra $10,000 per year won't make much difference (especially when you factor in taxes).

In any case, don't accept the offer without probing more deeply.

Alternative 1: Without communicating surprise or concern, ask what factors were evaluated to arrive at the salary.

Alternative 2: Confirm the details of the benefits package such as vacation and health insurance. Then, take a day or two to ask professionals outside the company what they would expect the salary to be.

Alternative 3: With or without mentioning the company's name, place an anonymous call to the human resources department of a competitor. Ask what they might expect the salary range for your position to be and why. To avoid being too specific, you might phrase this as a multiple choice question using salary ranges.

Unacceptable offers

For any negotiation to be successful, both parties must see the deal as fair. If you're unhappy with the stated salary, say so. Take some time to weigh the particulars of the offer and then be polite and forthright in informing them that the salary is below your expectations.

If you know you're worth more, stand firm. The company may have given you a low figure to see how you would react. If it becomes apparent that the company cannot meet your minimum salary requirements, use the opportunity to discuss alternatives. It might be possible to balance compensation objectives through performance-based bonuses, vacations, and other benefits.

By defending your value and taking time to understand the company's financial constraints, you might discover that the position is less challenging or growth-oriented than you hoped. It's also possible the company is just plain cheap. In any event, this is the time to find out.

Get it in writing

Once you reach an agreement, make sure all details are in writing. If no one has said anything about sending a formal offer letter, it is perfectly legitimate to ask for one. In all likelihood, the company has a standard letter that can be tailored to the specifics of your offer. At the same time, human resources personnel will probably send a new employee handbook with information about company policies and procedures.

If the company doesn't take the initiative to put the offer in writing, you should. If possible, hand-deliver it. The letter should include the key parts of the agreement including salary, vacation, bonus, profit sharing, and insurance. More specifically, it should highlight any agreements you reached that were beyond the scope of a typical offer. For example, if you successfully negotiated for a health club membership, company car, parking privileges, or a six-month salary review, make sure that's spelled out in the letter. Unlike a verbal agreement, a written agreement won't be subject to the selective memory of people who may not be around in six months to honor it. And, by the way, congratulations!

Improving Your
Technique and Yourself

tive criticism, and learning from interviews. We'll also explore the importance of recruiting and working with mentors because there is no better way to accelerate your personal and professional development.

Take the
Right Approach

Now that you've established a solid foundation of self-awareness and an extensive inventory of ways to demonstrate your potential, it's time to think about methods for polishing your overall presentation. This chapter will cover a variety of strategies for overcoming nervousness, seeking construc-

Job hunting can be an intense, highly competitive, ego-battering experience. It's even more stressful for energetic, motivated people, who are likely to have high expectations that can heighten disappointment as well as contribute to success. To avoid unnecessarily high expectations, commit yourself to a course of action rather than a specific outcome. For example, make the goal of your job search personal growth rather than a particular job offer. That way, you can emerge a stronger, more confident person even if you don't get the job you think you want most. Developing this attitude is as challenging as it is helpful because it requires a sincere desire for self-improvement and the ability to appreciate your value as a human being.

A sincere desire for self-improvement is the litmus test for potential. No matter who you are, there will always be room for improvement. This is one reason even the world's greatest athletes have coaches and mentors.

Find a Mentor

mentor: *an experienced and trusted counselor* (Oxford English Dictionary)

This definition is only partially true. Trusted counselor? Yes. Experienced? Maybe, but maybe not. A mentor isn't your on-the-job personal trainer, and he or she is more than just a corporate therapist to get you through the hard times. Ideally, a mentor is a trusted coach, a devil's advocate, and a cheerleader.

Typically, although the best coach is strong where the person seeking assistance is weak, experience is not a prerequisite. Think about it. When Olympic diver Greg Louganis began practicing reverse 3½ somersaults on the three-meter board, there wasn't a single person on the planet who had

ever done it. Yet he still had a coach. The same is true for Michael Jordan. Before his final season, Jordan said he would play one more year, but only with Phil Jackson as his coach.

To believe—even for a moment—that you or I don't need coaching is as dangerous as it is arrogant. Corporate layoffs—so common they no longer make headlines—serve as almost daily reminders that employees are discretionary expenses who must continually demonstrate value.

Where do you need coaching?

Determining this requires self-awareness, objectivity, and focus. Together, these traits will enable you to answer the following questions:

- Where am I?
- What am I working toward?
- What steps am I taking?
- Where are the gaps in my professional development?
- In what areas do I need to improve?
- Am I committed to improving?
- And, most important, Am I coachable?

Once you have answers for these questions congratulate yourself. The hard part is done.

For me, cost-containment and budgeting have never been among my favorite tasks. So when I began to identify my weak links, I made sure at least one of my mentors was a financial whiz. The second of my current mentors has a strong marketing background. I sought this person's counsel not because marketing is another of my weak links. On the contrary, it's one of my strengths. However, I am not—and never will be—the one, all-powerful, all-knowing marketing force in the universe. There will always be room for improvement. Given my goal of helping people through seminars and presentations, my other mentors are professional speakers who have made a business of motivational speaking and training.

Recruiting coaches

Finding a mentor isn't as hard as recognizing you need one. For each area in which you feel you need improvement, ask yourself:

Whom do I most admire and respect for his or her ability in this area?

It might come as a surprise, but you don't have to know or be friends with someone to ask for his or her help. When you locate a suitable candidate, explain who you are, what you're working toward, and why you admire him or her. Then ask the person to help you develop your skills. Most people are so flattered to be asked for advice that they are more than willing to help.

If the person declines, don't hear "No," hear "Next." There are several billion people on the planet, and some of them have comparable skills. Find them. If you don't know who these people are, ask. Ask the person who declined, ask your boss, ask your room-

mate, ask everyone, and keep asking until you know.

Challenge yourself to look beyond your current company for coaching. As long as you don't compromise company confidentiality or security, you won't have a problem. Developing a diverse network of coaches is also a good way to build a reputation for being sincere, coachable, and committed to improvement. These rare qualities are among the most valuable you can offer a company.

Keep in mind, however, that all of this is meaningless if you, as the person being coached, don't make yourself available for coaching. It's nice to have a mentor, but he or she won't do much good if you don't call, set objectives, establish time lines, and stick to your plan. And, in addition to having a plan, be open-minded, and be grateful for the constructive criticism you receive.

Self-Improvement Techniques

Seek constructive criticism

With the possible exception of the terminally unhappy and dissatisfied, most people are not comfortable vocalizing criticism. Given this, you can help your coach or mentor—or anyone you can learn from, for that matter—by creating a space in which people can view their insight as helpful rather than critical. To help people feel comfortable sharing constructive criticism, approach them with genuine curiosity, openness, and sincerity.

As you listen to what others have to say about you, be courteous and grateful. If the feedback surprises you, explore its origin. To avoid appearing confrontational or defensive, imagine yourself as an objective third party searching for the truth. It won't always be easy to hear the uncensored impressions of others. That's why you have to be extremely careful to avoid sounding angry or agitated. For example, if you interrupt or ask, "What do you mean by that?" with a defensive tone of voice, the person will probably become uncomfortable. Instead, challenge yourself to smile as you probe further, saying, perhaps, "That's interesting. Help me understand what led to that impression."

In some cases, the other person's experiences may have had a greater impact on their interpretation than your actual behavior. It's also possible that the impressions were consistent with your actions but inconsistent with your intentions. This is the time to find out.

You might probe even further by asking friends, family, and acquaintances what they see as your strengths and weaknesses. Just because you haven't asked, doesn't mean they haven't thought about it.

Develop your talents

The desire to improve yourself does not have to relate to a weakness in your character or ability. Instead, this desire might manifest

> No amount of self-improvement can make up for a lack of self-acceptance. —*Robert Holden*

itself in your commitment to projects, hobbies, and other extracurricular activities.

One interviewer shocked me when he said that it was my commitment to piano lessons—more than any other experience—that most strongly demonstrated my potential. He was genuinely impressed that I had spent over a year learning to play the first movement of Beethoven's "Grande Sonata Pathétique." He loved the fact that I had that kind of dedication as a senior in high school. Actually, I don't think dedication is rare. Hobbies and interests inspire far greater passion. People just don't think to sell themselves on it.

Dealing with Rejection

It's important to remember that your value as a person is absolutely separate from your ability to compete successfully against others. It's only natural to want to be the best. Just be comfortable with the fact that there will always be people of greater and lesser ability. The only person for you to outperform is yourself.

A single important rejection or series of disappointments can humble even the most confident and secure person. It's always dis-

> Fear is the thief of dreams.
> —*Ronald Thornton*
>
> I realized early on that success was tied to not giving up. Most people in this business gave up and went on to other things. If you simply didn't give up, you would outlast the people who came in on the bus with you.
> —*Harrison Ford*

heartening to know you haven't met someone else's expectations. Nevertheless, take rejection for what it is—a fact of life. For people who never appreciate their self-worth, rejection is a license to quit. For others, it is an excellent opportunity to reassess strengths, weaknesses, and goals.

Follow up on rejections

Not long ago I spoke with a recent college graduate, Jay, who had just been rejected by fifteen medical schools. He was crushed because the year before, ten schools had rejected him. Looking at his credentials and college transcript, Jay appeared to have all the right qualifications: perfect marks in every class, interesting extracurricular activities, and solid application essays. Despite this, he didn't get a single acceptance letter in two years. To my surprise, Jay never thought to get feedback after his first rejections. Instead, he spent countless hours

and hundreds of dollars repeating the same mistakes.

Had Jay taken time to understand the issue, I'm sure he would have been able to find a way to address it. Unfortunately, like many people, Jay never imagined that a recruiter would take the time to discuss an individual application. The fact is, any organization that charges an application fee owes you at least that much. Otherwise, what assurance would you have that they didn't cash the check and throw the paperwork away? An application fee that doesn't buy a little constructive criticism should be refunded. Don't be shy or afraid to ask for criticism that will only help you in the long run.

The same holds true for job interviews. But in this case, since the company doesn't have any obligation to help you, in order to receive feedback you have to approach the situation very diplomatically. Unlike a graduate school, which charges you to apply, the potential employee doesn't pay an application fee. The company views the interview as an investment in its future success, and once it's determined that it isn't interested in hiring you, it isn't likely to dedicate any more resources to you as a candidate. Nevertheless, if you can find a person with whom you had good chemistry, you may be able to get the insight you need to learn from the experience.

You might begin, for example, by saying that you understand and respect the decision that there wasn't a good fit. Having said this up front, the person will be less likely to be defensive because you won't come across as confrontational. Then you can say you're

> There can be no real freedom
> without the freedom to fail.
>
> —*Eric Hoffer*
>
> The greatest mistake you can make in
> life is to be continually fearing that
> you will make one.   —*Elbert Hubbard*

committed to working in the industry, explain that you have interviews in the near future (even if nothing has been scheduled), and ask what you can do to improve your chances of being hired. More specifically, ask if there are any areas where you can be more convincing. But remember, this is not an opportunity to get defensive, and it isn't a second chance to sell yourself. Use this strictly as an opportunity to gather information. All the while, be extremely appreciative of whatever you learn.

If the conversation goes well, ask the person to suggest the names of people in the industry you might contact. In any case, be sure to send a thank-you note.

Overcoming Nervousness

For many, job hunting in general and interviews in particular never seem to get easier. Even the words themselves can inspire fear. While it's understandable to be nervous

before an interview, you don't want to be so nervous that you can't relax. Just remember, it's your relaxed and enthusiastic self that employers are looking to hire. Show them that person.

Solid preparation may be the best natural cure for nervousness. If you've done a comprehensive self-analysis and matched your skills to the company's needs, there is no question you can't handle. However, there are always a few unsettling moments in an interview, and you should be prepared to encounter one or more of them.

When your mind goes blank

If you've taken a moment to think about a question and you still don't have an answer, be honest and inform the interviewer that you're struggling to come up with an answer. Then ask him or her to rephrase the question. Honesty is important for a number of reasons. First, it can loosen the vice grip of embarrassment and uncertainty. Second, it buys time to think about the question. Finally, honesty communicates sincerity.

Overcoming insecurity

If insufficient preparation is not a factor in your nervousness, you might be facing a more general insecurity. If so, that's what you need to confront.

The insecurity I felt in interviews extended to public speaking, group meetings, and other events in which I felt vul-

> When one door of happiness closes, another one opens; but often we look so long at the closed door that we do not see the one that has been opened for us.
> —*Helen Keller*

nerable to criticism. I didn't realize that the expectations I wasn't living up to were my own. This finally became clear when a concerned friend asked, "What, exactly, do you tell yourself before an interview?" It's when I began to face the insecurity and looked inward that I understood its origin.

All of my life, I've done well in almost every pursuit—at least the ones I considered important. Even graduate school wasn't especially difficult for me. Unfortunately, by generalizing these experiences, I taught myself to expect that desire alone would lead to success. What I created was the perfect recipe for disappointment.

By punishing myself unnecessarily, I turned interviews and presentations into moments of sheer terror. The fear—and my ability to control it—seemed wholly unpredictable. Without warning I would either shake visibly or ramble energetically. Either way, I was difficult to follow. As a result, my presentations looked like panic attacks.

Recognizing the problem, I realized I had two alternatives. I could either forge my way through life dreading every presentation, or expose my insecurities to the world and drive them out of my life. Choosing the latter proved to be a wonderful and liberating experience.

Enrolling in the Dale Carnegie course in human relations and public speaking gave me the courage to accept another, more difficult challenge—improvisation classes at Second City Players' Workshop.

As seamlessly as possible, the players in an improv group establish the relationships and initiate activities based on suggestions from the audience. By watching, listening, and involving themselves fully, the players' attention naturally slips into the scene they're creating. To focus on the actions of the team and still be consumed by self-consciousness is literally impossible.

The same is true for interviewing. Involve yourself fully in the conversation and watch for nonverbal signals. If you do, you won't have any energy left to be nervous, and you may even enjoy yourself.

Trusting Your Intuition

One of the most important steps you can take to enhance your long-term happiness and satisfaction is to develop, trust, and follow your intuition. This means learning to listen to your body and the important signals it provides. How many times have you heard yourself or others say, "I knew I shouldn't have done that. I had a bad feeling about it from the start." Warnings like this are often experienced as a sick or uncomfortable feeling in the abdomen. That's why people refer to this as a "gut feeling."

I have come to believe that our minds, bodies, and spirits have a whole communication system relating to intuition that isn't limited to those gut feelings. Once you become tuned in to the "network" Mona Lisa Schulz refers to in her book *Awakening Intuition*, you open up unlimited potential for insight and healing.

One of the best ways to develop your intuition is to keep a dream journal. I started doing this several years ago after reading *The Artist's Way* by Julia Cameron. The book recommended writing a few pages every morning about anything to promote creativity, but I found myself writing more and more about the dreams I had the night before. Since then, I have faithfully kept a dream journal *almost* every day. I've had two incredible dreams that proved to be prophetic, the one I will tell you about I had while working at the Chicago Board of Trade. In the dream I was shown a variety of vivid images and given the message that I

needed to write two books. The dream was so startling that I woke up and instantly wrote it down. At the time, I laughed it off because I had no intention of writing a book. Just three months later I began the first book.

Another way to tap into the power of intuition and similar forms of guidance is to pay attention to coincidences. In the book *Synchronicity and You*, Frank Joseph describes the many varieties of synchronous events as well as clues to interpret your own experiences. Through the suggested journal-keeping, I have realized how "meaningful coincidence" is an important part of my life.

Richard Brasser, a good friend, is a great example of someone who has changed his life using dreams and intuition. Richard used this intuition (and a lot of hard work) to change his life and career. Richard's story—in his own words—is a fitting way to end this chapter and the book.

Intuition and a Dream Job

There have been many lessons I have learned in my life. Some very difficult and some easy. But this one had the most impact.

After graduating from college with a degree in psychology, I set out into the world to discover my dream job. I had several talents, but no real goals or direction. I moved to Chicago, where I worked as a waiter, a drummer in a band, and an insurance salesman. I even worked for Orkin, promoting the company and the effect their products have on roaches—which I'm embarrassed to say included a day in a roach suit!

Overall, I was having a good time, but I was frustrated because I still wasn't sure what I wanted to do. I thought after one year in the city, something would have jumped out at me, but it didn't. I spent the next several months very frustrated and down about my search for the perfect job. I would spend hours thinking and researching to learn about jobs that might appeal to me and fields I might be qualified to pursue, but I wasn't getting anywhere. One day it hit me. I was waiting for my dream job to fall at my feet or hit me on the head. I spent endless hours thinking about what I wanted to do, but very little time actively talking to people. That's when I discovered my most important lesson: The person standing next to you in the elevator, at the store, or on the street can change your life.

I redirected my efforts and created a new plan of attack. I would talk to everyone. I'd been so frustrated that the hesitation I used to feel about potentially annoying people drifted away. I was determined to get little pieces of information from everyone. Cab drivers, businessmen, photographers, window washers, friends, teachers, even bums on the street. And believe it or not, I learned something from every single person I met. This new approach was changing my life.

Although I learned a great deal and enjoyed many wonderful opportunities, I still hadn't identified my dream job. Two years later, I moved to Miami Beach because it was a little nicer than winters in Chicago, and my sister, who worked in the fashion industry, was living there. I had always loved golf, so I went to the local course to ask if they needed help. They did, but I had to start as a ranger, the guy who drives around the course all day making sure no one plays too slowly or breaks any course rules. It wasn't exactly an exciting or challenging job, but it did give me the opportunity to play for free. And that I did. Every day I practiced and played and eventually became a pretty good golfer.

That's when I seriously considered a career in the golf business. I knew it would be a challenge because there weren't too many industries I knew less about, but I had passion and determination. I continued to talk with everyone, especially around the golf course, but I still didn't have any major breakthroughs.

Then, one night when I was working late at the course and feeling so tired that all I could think about was heading home and going to sleep, one of the golf company sales reps came in to talk with our head golf pro. I'd heard that these reps had some of the best jobs in golf, but I also heard they didn't like talking about it or helping people find out about opportunities. Since the guy didn't look particularly friendly, I walked right past him, through the pro shop doors, and out the front entrance to the club. Then I stopped dead in my tracks. I had a strong feeling that this was a person I really needed to talk to. It sounds dramatic, but I made myself turn around and go back in the pro shop to ask him every question I could think of.

The sales rep turned out to be a nice guy. He told me he graduated from a place called the San Diego Golf Academy, a two-year business school that specializes in the golf industry. I was surprised to hear that there was a school like that in existence. Looking back, this one moment and this one stranger changed my life more dramatically than anyone. I don't remember his name or even what company he represented, but I do remember that he sent me down a path that led to my dream job.

After learning more about the academy, I decided to apply. Two years later, I graduated and began playing on professional tours around the world. To my delight, I discovered that my true passion is teaching. I love to help people learn to play the game I love. I now own a golf school in Charlotte, North Carolina, called Targeted Golf Learning Center, and I'm thankful every day for the long and twisted path life lays before us. We may not be able to see where it's leading us, but as long as we keep moving forward, it leads somewhere wonderful.

Recommended Reading

Professional Development

In many respects, personal and professional development are closely related. Productivity and personal finance are just two of the areas where significant crossover exists. That's why I have listed a number of books that focus on this aspect of personal development.

Julia Cameron with Mark Bryan. *The Artist's Way: A Spiritual Path to Higher Creativity*. New York: G.P. Putnam's Sons, 1992.

A well-thought-out, effective method to help you nurture and develop your own creativity.

George S. Clason. *The Richest Man in Babylon*. New York: Penguin Books USA Inc., 1995.

A beautifully crafted, inspiring parable about getting out of debt and building wealth. The principles are extremely straightforward and, with a certain amount of discipline, easy to apply. If you have even the slightest difficulty saving money or getting out of debt, I urge you to read this book.

Rita Emmett. *The Procrastinators Handbook: Mastering the Art of Doing It Now*. New York: Walker & Company, 2000.

Written by a reformed procrastinator, this book is sure to inspire everyone who has projects they've been putting off indefinitely. I had the privilege of seeing Rita speak so I know firsthand how motivating she is. Rita definitely knows what she's talking about.

Melissa Everett. *Making a Living While Making a Difference: The Expanded Guide to Creating Careers with a Conscience*. Gabriola Island, British Columbia, Canada: New Society Publishers, 1999.

A wonderful book with countless real-life examples of people who have created careers based on their highest values. A must read for anyone committed to having a positive impact on the world.

Shakti Gawain. *Creative Visualization*. San Rafael, California: New World Library, 1978.

This is a step by step description of the meditations, exercises, and affirmations that are the basis for creative visualization. The process is often used for personal growth, health, and relaxation. A heart transplant patient I know used these techniques to deal with pain.

Napoleon Hill. *Think and Grow Rich*. New York: Penguin Books USA Inc., 1972.

Loaded with inspirational stories of people who overcame difficulties on the road to financial independence and prosperity. This book explores the power of imagination, creativity, and focus as it applies to goal setting and creating the life you desire. Don't be put off by the title. It's not a get-rich-quick type book.

Christopher Hoenig. *The Problem Solving Journey: Your Guide for Making Decisions and Getting Results*. Cambridge, Massachusetts: Perseus Publishing, Inc., 2001.

Considering the emphasis that many employers place on recruiting people with strong problem-solving skills, this book should be on the reading list for every serious job hunter and budding executive. Hoenig describes the six essential components of effective problem solving, beginning with generating the proper mind-set and attitude through creating solutions and delivering results. What I like best about this book is the wealth of real world examples that extend well beyond the business world. *The Problem Solving Journey* will help you maximize your own problem-solving skills.

Michael Landes. *The Back Door Guide to Short Term Job Adventures*. Berkeley, California: Ten Speed Press, 1997.

This is a great resource for recent graduates and anyone looking to travel, explore, and make money at the same time. This book is loaded with internships, seasonal jobs, overseas jobs, and volunteer opportunities. Separate chapters are devoted to the environment, artistic adventures, the great outdoors, adventure careers, camps and resorts, and socially responsible opportunities.

Laurie Lewis. *What to Charge: Pricing Strategies for Freelancers and Consultants*. Putnam Valley, New York: Aletheia Publications, 2000.

A valuable resource for freelancers and other self-employed professionals. This book provides great insights about analyzing projects, researching what other freelancers charge, developing contracts, negotiating, setting fees, and countless other topics of interest to people who work for themselves.

David Ogilvy. *Ogilvy on Advertising*. New York: Random House, 1987.

This is the book that got me excited about advertising. Ogilvy's colorful style and insight made me wish that I could have lived through his years at Ogilvy & Mather.

Catherine Ponder. *The Dynamic Laws of Prosperity*. Marina del Rey, California: Devorss & Company, 1985.

The author, a minister in the nondenominational Unity faith, is an inspirational writer who uses countless personal examples and case studies to get her points across. Not long after I read this book, I witnessed its effectiveness in my own life. The principles and affirmations definitely work. Extremely motivational.

Kelly Reno. *The 101 Best Freelance Careers*. New York: Berkeley Publishing Group, 1999.

A valuable source of ideas for anyone considering self-employment as a freelancer. Often, when people think of freelance professionals, they think of writers, graphic designers, and other creative types who work for a variety of different employers on a project basis. However, this book will open your mind to ninety-nine other opportunities you may never have considered.

Terry Savage. *The Savage Truth on Money*. New York: John Wiley & Sons, Inc., 1999.

This wonderful book is a valuable resource for people committed to getting out of debt, planning for their future, and anyone tempted to postpone financial planning indefinitely. Unlike the dreadfully boring financial books that clutter bookstore shelves, *The Savage Truth* is fascinating, well-written, and inspiring.

Marsha Sinetar. *Do What You Love and the Money Will Follow: Discovering Your Right Livelihood*. New York: Dell Publishing, 1987.

This is a great book that will help you to better understand and express yourself through your work. Having worked as a headhunter, I know for a fact that more and more people are growing dissatisfied with traditional nine-to-five jobs. A steady paycheck is no longer enough. An increasing number of people also want to feel they're making a difference and growing personally. If you find yourself in this group, read this book.

More Great Reading

Sylvia Boorstein. *It's Easier Than You Think: The Buddhist Way to Happiness*. New York: HarperCollins, 1997.

If you don't have a background or interest in Eastern philosophy, this would be an easy book to pass over. Don't let that happen. Thanks to Sylvia Boorstein's matter-of-fact style, the chapters are clear, memorable, and concise. The insights are universal. And the path to happiness is accessible. To put it another way, enlightenment probably isn't what you think it is.

Tom Brown, Jr. *Awakening Spirits, Grandfather, The Journey, The Quest, The*

Search, The Science and Art of Tracking, Tom Brown's Field Guides (a series of books on wilderness survival), *The Tracker, The Vision, The Way of the Scout.* New York: Berkley Publishing Group, 1978 to present.

In one of life's great synchronicities, I heard about Tom Brown's books from a guy I met when I switched planes at the last minute and took an earlier flight from Colorado to Chicago. Among the many things we had in common was a love for the outdoors. Saying only that I "absolutely had to read it," he told me to go to the bookstore the next day and buy *The Vision.* I devoured that book and eleven of Tom's other sixteen books in the next few months.

When Tom was eight years old, he met Stalking Wolf, an eighty-three-year-old Lipan Apache. Stalking Wolf, or Grandfather as he was called, never lived in civilization. At a young age, Grandfather left his tribe, which lived in the mountains of northern Mexico, and spent over sixty years wandering across North America and South America. When they met, Tom was collecting fossils by a riverbed in the Pine Barrens of New Jersey. Grandfather recognized Tom from a vision he'd had as a young man. Knowing that he was meant to teach Tom the ways of the earth, Grandfather stayed in the Pine Barrens for eleven years teaching Tom everything he knew about the earth, wild edible and medicinal plants, tracking, spirituality, and the Sacred Silence (a form of meditation).

Tom now runs a tracking, nature, and wilderness survival school called The Tracker. I have been fortunate to attend his Standard Course as well as a specialty tracking course in Search and Rescue. To say that Tom's work has deepened my appreciation of life, nature, and our place in the world would be an understatement. Read his books. Attend his classes. It will change your life.

Jack Canfield and Mark Victor Hansen. *The Aladdin Factor.* New York: Berkley Publishing Group, 1995.

An outstanding book about the power of asking for exactly what we want in every area of our lives. Includes some great goal-setting exercises as well.

Jack Canfield and Mark Victor Hansen. *Chicken Soup for the Soul: 101 Stories to Open the Heart and Rekindle the Spirit.* Deerfield Beach, Florida: Health Communications, 1993.

A collection of anecdotes about the life-changing differences we can make in someone's life—sometimes without realizing it. These books deepened my appreciation for the people who have helped to shape my life. With each paragraph, my desire to have the same impact on others also grew. The stories are so thought-provoking (and short—one to two pages) that I often read one in the morning and another before I go to bed. The sequels are equally good.

Dale Carnegie. *How to Stop Worrying and Start Living.* New York: Simon & Schuster, 1985.

A wonderful collection of techniques to eliminate the worry in your life. These true stories of overcoming stress, trauma, life- and career-threatening experiences are both memorable and inspirational. Although I read it almost six years ago, I remind myself of these techniques regularly.

His Holiness the Dalai Lama and Howard C. Cutler, M.D. *The Art of Happiness: A Handbook for Living.* New York: Riverhead Books, 1998.

An amazing book about human nature and relating more effectively and meaningfully with others. I found the sections on dealing with anger especially practical and valuable. It's nice to know there are people alive today as wise, loving, and compassionate as the Dalai Lama.

Viktor E. Frankl. *Man's Search For Meaning.* New York: Pocket Books, 1998.

Frankl discusses his own struggle as a prisoner in the Nazi death camps during World War II. As a psychiatrist and survivor, he examines the role of motivation and the human desire to find meaning in existence—even when that existence defies understanding. I can only echo the thoughts of my college psychology professor who said, "Anyone who even pretends to be educated should have read this book."

Debbie Ford. *The Dark Side of the Light Chasers: Reclaiming Your Power, Creativity, Brilliance, and Dreams.* New York: Riverhead Books, 1998.

An amazing book that will help you understand and learn from those aspects of yourself that you've worked hard to suppress. One of the most useful and helpful books I've ever read.

John Gunther. *Death Be Not Proud: A Memoir.* New York: Harper & Row, 1997.

A true story about the author's son, Johnny Gunther, who died at age seventeen of a brain tumor. Courage, faith, patience, perspective, and intelligence are words that only begin to capture the spirit of this book.

Frank Joseph. *Synchronicity & You: Understanding the Role of Meaningful Coincidence in Your Life.* New York: HarperCollins, 1999.

An enlightening book that breaks down meaningful coincidences and synchronicity into seventeen distinct categories ranging from dream, and premonitions to enigmas, warnings, guidance, and transformational experiences. After reading it, I started my own synchronicity journal to keep track and categorize the meaningful coincidences in my own life.

Carol Kruckeberg. *What Was Good About Today.* Seattle, Washington: Madrona Publishers.

A moving story about the author's eight-year-old daughter Sara. From the initial diagnosis of leukemia to her untimely death, Sara's spunk and positive energy rarely wavered. Despite her pain and prognosis, Sara and her family finished every day by answering the title's question, "What was good about today?" Deeply moving, yet hopeful.

Dan Millman. *The Way of the Peaceful Warrior*. Tiburon, California: H.J. Kramer, Inc., 1980

In this engaging story of self-discovery, Dan befriends a gas station attendant named Socrates who, through a series of late night conversations, becomes his mentor. With wit, wisdom, compassion, and a collection of bizarre experiences, Socrates helps Dan replace his inner confusion and cynicism with peace and understanding. This book is to emotional and personal development what The Celestine Prophecy is to the forces at work in the universe.

Kameel Nasr. *The World Up Close: A Cyclist's Adventures on Five Continents*. Bedford, Massachusetts: Mills & Sanderson.

This is the story of the author's 40,000 mile bicycle trek across the globe. Even more memorable than Nasr's descriptions of the countries are his insights about the people. For all of their cultural barriers, Nasr and the people he encountered found ways to communicate and enjoy each other's differences without relying on language, laws, or government. This book is as much about human relations as it is about adventure. After traveling through North and South America, India, Thailand, Japan, Africa—seventy countries in all—Nasr reached this conclusion:

> The biggest obstacle facing travelers is not dishonest people or wild animals or bad roads; it is not disease or food or bad water or diverse languages.

> Problems make travel an adventure which can, depending on a mixture of the traveler's ability and attitude and luck, enrich the traveler's life. The biggest obstacle to travelers is government.

Roger von Oech. *A Whack on the Side of the Head: How You Can Be More Creative*. New York: Warner Books.

A fun and involving book that examines ways to stimulate your creative potential. Loaded with great questions, puzzles, stories, and mental challenges.

James Redfield. *The Celestine Prophecy*. New York: Warner Books, 1993.

An adventure of discovery and understanding that revolves around the search for a series of nine manuscripts. Each describes an insight essential to understanding the nature of life itself and our place on this planet. If nothing else, you will pay more attention to coincidences.

I know so many people with strong and opposite feelings about this book that I must also include a word of caution. This is not a literary masterpiece. If you are a critical reader, don't let your feelings about the writing or story line camouflage the value of this work.

John Robbins. *Diet for a New America*. Tiburon, California: H.J. Kramer, Inc., 1987.

If anyone ever had a vested interest in maintaining America's appetite for processed food, it would have been John Robbins, heir to the Baskin & Robbins ice cream empire. Instead, Robbins has dedicated his life to exploring the links between diet, health, and the environment. While this book may not turn you into a vegetarian, it will absolutely make you think twice about nutrition and the foods you consume. As antibiotics, irradiation, and genetic engineering play an ever-increasing role in the world's food production, you owe it to yourself to read what the food industry doesn't want you to know.

Lloyd E. Shefsky. *Entrepreneurs Are Made, Not Born: Secrets from 200 Successful Entrepreneurs*. New York: McGraw-Hill.

A factual and inspirational reference for anyone who has ever considered starting his or her own business. This book opens the mind to different ways of thinking. By the time I read the last page, I had three solid, original ideas for starting my own company.

Neale Donald Walsch. *Conversations with God: An Uncommon Dialogue* (Books 1, 2, and 3), *Friendship with God*, and *Communion With God*. Charlottesville, Virginia: Hampton Roads Publishing.

Whether or not you accept Walsch's assertion that he maintains an ongoing dialogue with God, anyone even remotely interested in God and/or spirituality would find these books thought provoking in a good way. Of particular interest is the discussion about both the validity and the shortcomings of all organized religions.

Brian Weiss, M.D. *Many Lives, Many Masters, Messages from the Masters, Only Love Is Real*, and *Through Time into Healing*. New York: Warner Books.

A conservative, analytical Yale-trained psychiatrist and former chairman of the Department of Psychiatry at Mount Sinai Medical Center, Weiss was not exactly a poster child for New Age thinking on past lives, spirituality, or anything even somewhat related. Nevertheless, during the course of one life-changing hypnotherapy session, Weiss took Catherine, his patient, back to her childhood without uncovering the cause of her anxiety. Dr. Weiss then asked Catherine to go back to the source of her trauma. Both were shocked when she began to have vivid recollections of a past life as a slave in ancient Egypt. Even more amazing, her symptoms improved dramatically. Having achieved similar results with other patients, Weiss could no longer deny the validity or effectiveness of the past life regression therapy. At great risk to his professional reputation, he has published these books to share his experiences and encourage dialogue. Absolutely fascinating reading.

About the Author

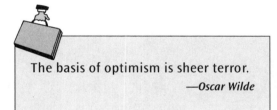

> The basis of optimism is sheer terror.
> —*Oscar Wilde*

Rob Sullivan is living proof that the exercises described in this book are effective. After more than eighty interviews and a humbling series of rejections in the ultra-competitive advertising industry, Rob uncovered the secrets of effective job hunting. With this knowledge, he reapplied to Leo Burnett—the agency that rejected him the year before—and earned a coveted spot in the company's Client Service Training Program. At Burnett, Rob worked as an account executive on the Philip Morris/Marlboro, McDonald's, and John G. Shedd Aquarium accounts. He also gained extensive experience as an interviewer and campus recruiter.

In 1994, Rob decided to pursue one of his other lifelong dreams—to become a trader at the Chicago Board of Trade. This gave him the opportunity to use the same job-hunting principles to reposition himself for a completely different career. Despite the fact that he had no formal experience, Rob earned a position with Cooper Neff & Associates—one of the premier options trading firms in the world. Although he no longer works on the trading floor, Rob is currently using this experience in his role as freelance writer and content provider for optionsXpress, an on-line brokerage firm specializing in options trading.

Through his own ongoing process of self-evaluation, Rob has also decided to dedicate his talents to "marketing that makes a difference." Helping job hunters, career changers, and companies is an important part of that objective. To this end, he currently speaks at colleges, universities, and companies, helping job hunters and recruiters alike. In addition, Rob works on a project basis with Carpenter Associates, Inc., a retained executive search firm. In his role as Senior Consultant, Rob has contact with hiring companies and candidates at all levels. From his perspective as a head-hunter, Rob continues to gain insight into the ways job hunters can market themselves even more effectively.

Rob has a B.A. in psychology from the College of the Holy Cross in Worcester, Massachusetts, as well as an M.S. in advertising from Northwestern University's Medill School of Journalism.